PENGUIN BOOKS

Cosmopolitan Guide to Working in Journalism and
Publishing

Suzanne King is an experienced print journalist who has worked
on a number of magazines, including *Cosmopolitan* (of which she is
a former Careers Editor), *SHE* and *Radio Times*. Now a freelance
writer and commissioning editor, she is also series editor of the
Cosmopolitan Careers Guides, author of *Cosmopolitan: How to Get
Ahead in Your Career* and co-author of the *Cosmopolitan Guide to the Big
Trip*, both of which are forthcoming in Penguin.

COSMOPOLITAN
Guide to Working in
Journalism and **Publishing**

SUZANNE KING

PENGUIN BOOKS

PENGUIN BOOKS

Published by the Penguin Group
Penguin Books Ltd, 27 Wrights Lane, London w8 5TZ, England
Penguin Books USA Inc, 375 Hudson Street, New York, New York 10014, USA
Penguin Books Australia Ltd, Ringwood, Victoria, Australia
Penguin Books Canada Ltd, 10 Alcorn Avenue, Toronto, Ontario, Canada M4V 3B2
Penguin Books (NZ) Ltd, 182–190 Wairau Road, Auckland 10, New Zealand

Penguin Books Ltd, Registered Offices: Harmondsworth, Middlesex, England

First published 1996
10 9 8 7 6 5 4 3 2 1

Set in 10.5/13pt Monotype Baskerville
Typeset by Datix International Limited, Bungay, Suffolk
Printed in England by Clays Ltd, St Ives plc

Contents

Acknowledgements

I'd like to thank all those who gave up the time to be interviewed for the book, both those who feature as case histories and those whose names don't actually appear in the text but who supplied valuable background information. Thanks, too, to Emma Dally for her patience and support, to Becky Leuws for research assistance, and to Rowena Young for being such an all-round star.

Chapter 1 / **Introduction**

No one knows exactly how many journalists there are in the UK but on one thing everyone agrees: there are always far more eager young hopefuls queuing up to join their ranks than there are jobs for them to fill. A MORI survey conducted annually among students shows that half of them are interested in a career in broadcasting and journalism, even though when it comes to public disapproval and dislike, journalists are right up – or down – there with politicians and estate agents. Competition for jobs is fierce, so to be successful journalists must be as determined, persistent and – rather unfairly – lucky as they are talented.

Many are attracted by what they see as a glamorous life – and it's true that working in the media *can* be glamorous at times. If you're lucky enough to work for a high-profile publication or programme, you may receive invitations to parties, tickets for films and plays, and free books. There may be perks such as press trips abroad, discount on fashion goods or samples of beauty products. Some media employers provide additional bonuses such as commission-free traveller's cheques, subsidized canteens and leisure facilities. Once you've made it to the top, there may be company cars, clothes allowances and generous bonuses.

However, behind any perks, which are by no means common to all media jobs, lies a lot of routine and menial work. Journalistic jobs are rarely 100 per cent creative: most involve an element of administrative and routine work and you must be prepared to do your share of this. Then there's the stress of working long, unpredictable and often unsociable hours and having to meet daily or weekly deadlines. You may have to work shifts, sometimes – especially in news journalism – round the clock, and you'll need understanding friends and family who won't take offence when you have to cancel social arrangements at the last minute.

Don't expect a mega pay packet either, especially when you're starting out. So many people are willing to start at the bottom that employers can get away with paying meagre salaries to keen young things. The image of journalists spending most of their day at long, boozy lunches is very far from the truth and if you wish to succeed you must be committed, determined and hard-working.

Journalism has become an increasingly insecure job area, too. In the past ten years or so, the media have been radically transformed by the effects of deregulation, technological advances, the decline of the trade unions, economic recession and increasing competition for market share and advertising revenue. Developments such as desktop publishing and electronic news gathering have had a huge impact and work practices have undergone major changes as a result. Permanent staff numbers have been cut back and the industry, television especially, is now heavily reliant on freelances. In such a time of upheaval, journalism is definitely *not* a career for anyone who craves stability. To survive, you'll need to be immensely adaptable, flexible in attitude, and able and willing to acquire new skills as they become necessary.

Still, however much journalists moan about their work (and many of them do), most wouldn't dream of swapping it. There is a tremendous buzz that comes from working with like-minded people, producing a programme or publication that you can be proud of. It can give you a real thrill to hear somebody on the bus talking about your programme, or see them reading your magazine. The stresses and frustrations of working under pressure help develop great camaraderie and team spirit. All the changes in the industry have also led to increased flexibility, so that entry to the media now is probably easier than ever before. Once you're in one branch, it's also easier to cross over into others, with many journalists beginning to move between books, magazines, newspapers, TV and radio, rather than spending all their working life in one field.

There's enough variety of jobs to find a niche that suits you. If you thrive on adrenalin, go to a daily paper or programme. If you prefer to take more time developing ideas, aim for a monthly magazine or book publishing. If you want flexible working hours, there is never a shortage of work for good freelances. You can do desk-bound work or you can be out and about every day. The jobs may be largely London-based but plenty of openings exist else-where on local newspapers and radio stations. A few magazines and book publishers are also based outside the capital. As English is an international language, there are opportunities to work abroad, too, and you'll find British journalists working all over the world, from New York to New Zealand.

Many people think of journalists as news reporters, but the job is far more wide-ranging than that and you could find yourself working in a number of different fields. The three main areas are:

Press: national and local newspapers and press agencies
Periodicals: consumer magazines (those which cater for their reader-ship's leisure time, e.g. women's titles, sports magazines, special interest and general magazines); and business/professional publications
Broadcasting: national and local radio and television

In addition, the editorial side of **book publishing** calls upon journalistic skills. Many journalists also move into press and public relations, which is dealt with in the *Cosmopolitan Guide to Working in PR and Advertising*. In all these fields, there are possibilities to work both on staff and as a freelance.

Although journalism is still a male-dominated world, change is coming. Women may still be few and far between at the highest levels, but numbers of female recruits into all sectors of the media have been growing and in some areas – consumer magazines and book publishing, for example – they outnumber men.

In the next three chapters of this book, we'll take you through the main areas in which journalists are employed, and look at the kind of careers available in print journalism, broadcasting and book publishing. Chapter 5 contains advice on carving a successful

'Journalism largely consists in saying "Lord Jones Dead" to people who never knew Lord Jones was alive.'
G.K. Chesterton, *The Wisdom of Father Brown*

'The journalist is partly in the entertainment business and partly in the advertising business.'
Claud Cockburn, *In Time of Trouble*

'Journalists say a thing that they know isn't true, in the hope that if they keep on saying it long enough it *will* be true.'
Arnold Bennett, *The Title*

'Journalism – an ability to meet the challenge of filling the space.'
Rebecca West, *New York Herald Tribune*

'Journalism: a profession whose business it is to explain to others what it personally does not understand.'
Lord Northcliffe

'The fact is . . . all the faults of the age come from Christianity and journalism.'
Frank Harris

'You cannot hope/To bribe or twist/Thank God! The British journalist/But seeing what/That man will do/Unbribed, there's no occasion to.'
Humbert Wolfe, *Punch*

'An editor: a person who knows precisely what he wants – but isn't quite sure.'
Walter Davenport

'An editor is one who separates the wheat from the chaff and prints the chaff.'
Attributed to Adlai Stevenson

'It is inexcusable for scientists to torture animals; let them make their experiments on journalists and politicians.'
Henrik Ibsen

career as a freelance. Chapters 6 and 7 will help you decide whether you've got what it takes to be a journalist and, if you have, talk you through the job-hunting process. You'll find a brief glossary of media jargon in Chapter 8, a detailed guide to some of the main journalism training courses in Chapter 9, and, in Chapters 10 to 13, all the addresses you'll need to get you started in your search for a job. Finally, Chapters 14 and 15 suggest trade publications and further reading to give you a more in-depth knowledge of your chosen field.

Chapter 2 / **Newspapers and Magazines**

For years, people have been predicting the death of print journal-ism and anticipating the day when newspapers and magazines will be supplanted by electronic media. Certainly, the print media can't react as quickly to events as radio and TV, but they score over broadcast media in the detail and analysis they can provide. The amount of information contained in a typical three-minute radio news bulletin, for instance, would take up no more than ten or eleven column inches in a newspaper. Newspaper and maga-zine readers also have the advantage of being able to pick and choose what they read, when and where, and how quickly.

None the less, newspaper sales have steadily declined, for a number of reasons, which include competition from other media, trends in the way people spend their leisure time and demographic shifts. In addition, the print industry has been hit with a sharp increase in the cost of paper, forcing companies to look for new ways to cut costs. The battle to attract and retain readers is there-fore fierce and newspaper publishers have employed a range of tactics to boost slipping circulations, from greatly reduced cover prices to games with large cash prizes. Magazine publishers, too, have been going all out to woo new readers, with incentives such as free books and supplements, and special subscriber clubs.

There have been closures and redundancies on many publica-tions, but a glance at one of the media guides confirms that the print media are still far from dead. The May 1996 issue of *BRAD* (see Chapter 15) revealed that UK readers support just under 2,000 newspapers (thirty-six nationals and 1,933 regional papers) and over 7,000 periodicals (2,424 consumer titles and 4,947 business titles). According to the Periodical Publishers' Association (PPA), the number of magazines published in the

UK has actually increased by 73 per cent in the past decade.

Publishers are also looking to futureproof themselves by investigating the possibilities of new technology. Already hundreds of newspapers and news services, including the *Financial Times*, the *Evening Standard*, the *Daily Telegraph*, the Mirror group and the *Independent* are available in some form on the Internet, and this is expected to grow to thousands over the next few years. Magazines, too, are starting to reproduce selected editorial on screen.

Press

Entry to newspaper journalism is now far more flexible and open than it was when the print unions ruled the roost, but it is still traditional to start on local papers and learn the trade there for a couple of years before getting a break into Fleet Street – still often used as a term for the national press although none of the newspapers has offices there any longer. The regional press is by far the biggest employer of newspaper journalists, and starting your career here will give you good all-round experience and the chance to try your hand at everything from court reporting to wedding write-ups. National papers are seen as strictly the province of qualified or experienced journalists.

News journalists are also employed by news agencies or press agencies, which provide a reporting service, press cuttings, news leads and photographs to newspapers and broadcasting organizations. Subscribers can then cut and/or rewrite a story to fit their style, and run it either with the agency's byline or 'from our own correspondent'. Being able to use material from an agency saves a newspaper having to maintain its own foreign correspondents or allows it to have people only in the major cities.

The largest and most famous agency is Reuters, with staff around the world. Other international agencies include Associated Press, UPI and Agence France Presse. Within the UK, the Press Association (PA), is the leader among domestic news agencies, although it is now facing increased competition from the relatively new UK News. Other press agencies provide a specialist service in, for example, sports reports or entertainment news.

Newspaper journalism is still very much male-dominated, especially in the so-called 'hard news' areas (news, politics, economics and leaders) and sport; at the moment, women are more likely to be found on the features desk. The first woman editor of a national newspaper was Wendy Henry, appointed editor of the *News of the World* in 1987 and, nearly a decade on, female editors of nationals are still thin on the ground. However, as more women line up at deputy, assistant and executive editor level, the next decade may see more changes.

Periodicals

When most people think of magazines, they picture the glossy women's and lifestyle titles, yet these make up only a fraction of the number of magazines published in the UK. Most periodicals are smaller trade and special-interest publications, with business titles outnumbering consumer titles by roughly two to one. They may specialize in anything from darts to dentistry, retailing to rambling; they may be produced in-house for the staff of large companies or put together by contract publishers for stores such as Marks & Spencer and Sainsbury's to sell. The great thing about this diversity is that you have the chance to work on a publication that reflects your personal interests.

Specialist magazines may have a circulation as small as a few hundred; the giants of the market (such as *Radio Times* and *Reader's Digest*) sell over a million. The size of staff varies hugely, too: a weekly listings title might have an editorial team of around eighty people; on a major women's monthly it would be around twenty to thirty, and on a specialist title, perhaps as few as one or two. The bigger the company, the brighter your promotion prospects, but the good thing about starting on a small magazine is that it gives you a chance to try your hand at everything, from writing and subbing to selling ad space or designing pages.

Magazines work much further ahead of publication than news-papers – anything from five to six weeks for a weekly to three months or more on a monthly magazine. Journalists have to get used to being out of sync with what's happening around them, think-ing about Christmas while everyone else is still concentrating on summer holidays and planning beach features when it's snowing.

The Job Descriptions

Precise job titles and descriptions vary from one publication to the next but here we've given an outline of some of the most common you could expect to find. As far as salaries go, national newspaper staff earn more than their magazine counterparts. A recent NUJ survey revealed that most magazine journalists' salar-ies were concentrated in the £15–£25,000 range, with a significant number earning under £15,000. By contrast, two-thirds of NUJ members working on national papers earned £30,000 or more, with only 8.3 per cent earning less than £15,000. On provincial papers, however, only 2.1 per cent earned over £30,000. National agencies' staff tended to get between £20,000 and £30,000.

Editor

There is as much variety in editors as there is in newspapers and magazines. Some are very 'hands-on', writing copy and taking a keen interest in every stage of putting each issue together, having a say in every headline, picture and story. Others delegate much of the day-to-day running to other senior editorial executives and take a more strategic role, spending time out and about represent-ing the publication and its views.

Whatever their style, all editors are ultimately responsible for the overall content, balance, tone, look and direction of their pub-lication. They have the final decision on all editorial matters – how important a story should be, how much space to allow it and where it should appear. That said, the amount of freedom editors have to run their publications in the way they want depends on the proprietor's policy. They also come under pressure from advertisement departments, who may try to influence or dictate editorial content or pagination, so they must be strong enough to fight their corner and defend editorial pages and integrity.

As well as working on current issues, editors have to be involved in the long-term planning of the publication and its direction, deciding on editorial policy and dreaming up ways to attract new readers and retain the loyalty of existing ones. However well respected an editor might be, she won't last long if the management think somebody else could boost the circulation higher.

Increasingly, editors are expected to act as ambassadors for their publication, giving radio and television interviews as often as possible, sitting on industry committees and generally doing anything that helps raise the publication's profile both within and outside the industry. No journalist works a nine-to-five day, but editors particularly are on call at all times and are expected to sacrifice much of their personal life and free time.

In newspapers, a key part of every day is the morning conference, when the editor gathers together the inner group or senior editorial executives, to discuss the contents for the next day's paper. Each department head (news editor, sports editor, features editor, women's editor, picture editor, etc.) presents ideas for the editor's approval. On magazines, too, much of an editor's day will be spent in meetings with other members of staff, looking at the art department's layouts, discussing ideas with the features department, approving models with the fashion team, etc. All department heads report to the editor, who is ultimately responsible for the personnel of the magazine, appointing staff, deciding on salaries and overseeing their work.

All editors of major titles have had solid journalistic experience but you do not necessarily need to be a superb writer to be a good editor. You should have a constant fund of original ideas, the ability to see them through and sound creative judgement. Good editors are creative and innovative people.

Kathy Watson

Age : **32**
Job : **Editor, *Woman's Realm* (weekly)**
Based : **London**
Salary : **'plenty'**
Qualifications : **BA (Hons.) English Literature**

'I started as editorial assistant with a trade press company, then became arts editor at *The Voice*. From there I went to BBC radio, then freelance for a year, then I went to *Bella* as commissioning editor. I joined *Woman's Realm* as features editor in 1992, became deputy editor, then acting editor and was appointed editor in 1995.

'I do all the obvious things: reading copy, choosing pictures, looking at layouts and working on the cover. I plan ahead with all the department heads, control the budget, and work out ways to promote the magazine. I also act as a representative for the magazine, giving presentations, talking to the ad and production departments, doing radio interviews. I like being involved in management but I'm happiest here in the office, working out an issue.

'You need stamina and resilience, because the hours are long and, on weeklies, the schedule is pulverizing. You're holding at least four issues in your head at one time – one you're planning, one you're reading copy for, one you're looking at layouts for, one you're reading proofs for. I could stay until twelve and I still wouldn't have cleared the work. And you need persistence: when you're chasing a story, you may have made twenty calls but it's making that twenty-first to get the right case history . . .

'Getting the first break is the key and you have to be quite unfussy about the first thing you do. Once you're in and you've done something, it's easier to get on to the next stage – a lot of jobs are got through contacts. It's extraordinary, though, how many people turn up for interviews without having even read the magazine. And I often feel that interviewees just aren't well informed or well read enough. The more you know, the better you do any job – people should carry on learning as much as they can. You can always tell the subs who are well read because they're much sharper about language.

'Once you've got your first job, you should ask if you can do more. A lot of people are good at doing what they're asked to do but don't show any kind of initiative. The very good people are a real find and employers will do a lot to keep them.'

Lyn Hughes

Age : **38**
Job : **Editor, *Wanderlust* (two-monthly)**
Based : **Windsor, Berkshire**
Salary : **'a fraction of what I used to earn outside publishing'**
Qualifications : **7 O levels; 2 A levels**

'I left school at eighteen and, after a spell in the Civil Service, joined the Mars Corporation where I stayed for twelve years. In my early thirties I took a break to spend a year going round the world. On my return I went freelance as a business analyst, but felt increasingly like a square peg in a round hole. The idea of starting a travel magazine came when my partner and I were on a plane reading the in-flight magazine and thinking what a load of dross it was.

'Everyone seems to think that as a travel editor I spend my time swanning around the world but the irony is that I rarely get to travel any more – I'd love to be out there doing it rather than reading and editing other people's articles. I do get offered free trips but I rarely have time to take them. What's more, the conventional organized press trip is anathema to *Wanderlust*. There are other, smaller perks, such as the books and some of the products that we review. However, the biggest perk is being involved in a job that I enjoy, covering a subject I love.

'My main role is to see that we get the right quality and style of content for the magazine, which means seeing it all the way through from planning and sourcing the material to writing, researching, editing and proofing. As a partner in the business I'm also involved in all business decisions. There's no room for ego and I often have to muck in answering the phones, stuffing envelopes or processing subscriptions.

'As the public face of the magazine, I network, attend functions and give lectures. Newspapers ask me to comment on topical issues and I regularly go on radio and sometimes television to talk about travel-related topics. A big time-consuming task is screening unsolicited articles (they have a one in 700 chance of being accepted) and dealing with correspondence from freelances. While there is no such thing as a typical day, the one constant is my postbag – it can take all morning to open and sort.'

Deputy Editor

A deputy must be able to do everything the editor does and stands in for holidays, sickness, etc. She may take on much of the day-to-day office administration and be the first point of contact for staff wanting to check ideas and copy. Together with the editor, she is responsible for the overall policy and direction of the magazine and must be creative and decisive. In many cases, a deputy will have skills that complement the editor's – if the editor spends much of the time out of the office being a public figurehead, the deputy must be a good hands-on manager; if the editor prefers to be more involved in the daily editorial work, the deputy may be the one dispatched to represent the publication in meetings and interviews.

A deputy editor on a trade magazine might earn in the region of £20,000 to £25,000; on a mainstream monthly, it might be more like £40,000 to £45,000. On a newspaper, salaries would be higher.

Managing Editor

The managing editor is a senior member of the editorial team. The title can mean different things, depending on the publication, but as a general rule, the job is largely administrative. Although a managing editor may be involved in some journalistic areas, her main role is to oversee the smooth running of the editorial office, freeing up the editor and deputy to concentrate on the creative side of things. She oversees the editorial finances, monitoring the different departments' costs and ensuring that budgets are not exceeded. It is also usually the managing editor who is responsible for doing the flatplan (see Chapter 9) and drawing up the production schedule, then liaising with the sub-editors and designers to ensure that deadlines are met. A managing editor must be tremendously organized, with a clear and logical mind, and confident enough to tackle journalists whose expenses are excessive or whose copy is consistently late – this is not a job for the shy and timid. They must also have good diplomatic and interpersonal skills, as they are often the first point of contact for any personnel or disciplinary problems.

Salaries for managing editors would probably be on a par with or slightly less than those of deputy editors.

News Editor

On a daily or weekly paper this is a senior position and carries with it long hours and lots of stress. While periodicals, with their long lead times, cannot be as topical as newspapers, news sections are also an important part of business magazines and of particular interest to their readers, so these titles employ news editors too.

The news editor is responsible for organizing the work of the news desk (department) and overseeing reporters and contributors, planning what goes in, which reporter does what and weighing up stories for importance. Every news desk keeps a diary of forthcoming events such as festivals, sports tournaments, significant anniversaries, local government meetings and exhibition openings, which is compiled from press releases, invitations, council calendars and court schedules. Every day, the news editor checks the diaries and allocates reporters to stories. There will also be stories that crop up without warning (accidents or deaths), so she has to reshuffle her resources to cope. Some days there will be more news than an editor knows what to do with; other days she and the reporters will have to work really hard to root it out.

The news editor must be constantly aware of breaking stories and monitor all the other news media to make sure their publication is not missing out on a big one. The job calls for someone who can think on her feet and work quickly and efficiently under extreme pressure. Like all journalists, you must also have a thorough understanding of legal pitfalls (libel, copyright, official secrets, etc.) and be alert to any potential problems in reporters' copy.

A news editor on a regional newspaper would probably earn between £17,000 and £25,000; on a national paper this could rise to upwards of £50,000.

Michelle Knott

Age : **29**
Job : **Technology News Editor, *New Scientist* (weekly)**
Based : **London**
Salary range : **£23–28,000**
Qualifications : **B.Sc. (Hons.) in Chemical Engineering; in-house training at Morgan-Grampian; 2 NVQs in journalism (news and features)**

'In my final year at university, I realized that I didn't want to be an engineer. Then I saw an advert for a publishing house that was recruiting technology graduates to work on its technical magazines. It was a revelation – I could use my engineering knowledge as a technical journalist. I trained on *Food Manufacture*, *The Engineer*, *Transport Week*, and then *Process Engineering*, where I eventually became associate editor. I moved to my present job in 1994.

'My main responsibility is to put together the four-page technology news section every week. On Tuesday, Wednesday and Thursday I commission stories from in-house reporters or freelance writers. Technology is such a broad field – Internet, genetic engineering, space, cars – there's no way I can be an expert in every aspect. When someone rings up with a story idea I often have to go away and do some research before I can decide whether to accept it or not. As the stories come in, I edit them into *New Scientist* style.

'All week, I'm working towards Friday, when the art department has to fit the stories together on page. I liaise with the picture department and illustrators, and decide which stories will go where and roughly how long they will be. On Monday morning I go through the page proofs, cutting stories to fit, making last-minute corrections, and writing headlines and captions. Sometimes I write stories myself.

'On a weekly magazine there is the constant pressure of deadlines – you can't really afford to have an off day. Being a commissioning editor is particularly stressful, partly because I'm relying on other people all the time. If they write a crap story, I'm the one who has to sort it out. I hate having to tell people when their work isn't suitable. There are some whose writing is just not good enough and that's a hard thing to say.

'Journalism is not something to go into to make your fortune – I'd be a lot richer today if I'd been a successful chemical engineer – but it's good fun. *New Scientist* covers such a vast range of subjects that it can never get boring and each week I learn so much.'

Melanie Swift

Age : **24**
Job : **News Editor, *LeisureWeek* (fortnightly)**
Based : **London**
Salary : **£17,500**
Qualifications : **2 A levels; 7 RSA exams in journalism-related subjects**

'Since the age of about 14, I wanted to be a journalist. After deciding not to go to university, I thought I'd try the secretarial route and got a job as PA to the editor of *LeisureWeek* in April 1990. I made it clear I wanted to be a journalist and, when my secretarial duties were done, offered to help out with research on features. I was promoted to reporter in 1991, senior reporter in 1993 and news editor in 1995.

'I'm busiest from Friday to Wednesday every other week. After scanning the papers for stories, I sort through the post and distribute it and the newspaper clippings to the reporters. At the beginning of the news week, we hold a meeting where everyone tells me what stories they're chasing. I plan what pages they might go on, then get on with chasing my own stories and getting regular updates from the other reporters. When stories are written, I read them on screen, check any points that seem unclear, then send them to our production editor. When I know which stories are definitely coming in, I decide how important they are and plan what position they should be on the page.

'We're encouraged to go out for lunch with contacts and to visit leisure operators, so there's plenty of opportunity to get out of the office and see a bit of the country. I've been on press trips to theme parks in Holland and Spain and I occasionally get free tickets to UK attractions and invitations to launches where there's free food and drink.

'I like the fact that I am pretty much free to organize my own time and go about things my own way so long as I produce the work within set deadlines. I particularly enjoy interviewing people for profile pieces – it's a great opportunity to exercise my natural nosiness – and I always feel really good if I manage to get a strong, exclusive news story, especially if it's when we're just closing the issue or are short of a good front-page lead story.'

Reporter

Every newspaper employs a team of reporters to gather the news. On small papers with limited resources, they must be able to write on any subject, from a major political story to a local wedding. On larger publications, they usually specialize in a particular area.

Sometimes they may be sent out on assignments, covering diary stories, which are known about in advance, or chasing up breaking news. Other times, they will be nosing out their own stories, calling up the emergency services (hospitals, police stations, fire stations, coastguards) and other contacts to find out what's happening: maintaining a good relationship with contacts is a vital part of a journalist's job. As well as initiating their own copy, reporters may also rewrite stories sent in by PRs or news agencies. The work is hugely varied: you could be out and about attending press conferences and following up leads, or spending days sitting through court sessions or council meetings. Some reporters work with a photographer; others are responsible for taking their own pictures.

Reporters must understand the public, be aware of its concerns and know what is relevant to their readership. On local papers, they would be expected to live in the area they cover and to keep their eyes and ears open at all times for stories. They must also have the ability to scent a story where none appears to exist and must have – or quickly develop – a thick skin: much of what makes news involves death and disaster and you have to be able to talk at the worst of times to people involved. Every reporter dreads what are known as 'death knocks' when they have to talk to the parents of a murdered child or the widow of a car-crash victim. People can also be hostile to journalists, especially if you're investigating something they'd prefer to hide.

Contrary to the popular image of the reporter as a sleazy hack, complete with grubby mac and dangling fag, you'll find that most are smartly turned out and are expected to look presentable at all times: they never know where they might have to go at a moment's notice or whom they might meet. Having said that, it depends on the area they work in – a music journalist, hanging out in pubs and clubs, would obviously not be expected to dress in the same way as a city reporter, dealing with bankers and stockbrokers.

A junior reporter on a regional paper could earn as little as £9,000 or £10,000; salaries for experienced reporters on national papers start at around £30,000.

Kate Watson-Smyth

Age : **28**
Job : **Reporter, *Birmingham Post* (daily)**
Based : **Birmingham**
Salary : ***c.* £16,000**
Qualifications : **3 A levels; NCTJ pre-entry course**

'I studied French at university but dropped out before graduating and went to teach English in Paris for three years. In 1992 I came back to England and worked as a communications officer for Oxfam. The following year I did a journalism course at Darlington and in 1994 I joined the *Birmingham Post* as a trainee reporter. I'd been on work experience here before and kept nagging for a job – and when they were interviewing for trainees they contacted me.

'You have to be a bit pushy when you get work experience: there's no point sitting quietly in a corner because you will be ignored and regarded as a wet blanket. Boundless enthusiasm for everything, however boring, is a winner.

'I generally start at 11 a.m. and make calls to fire, police and ambulance to see what has happened overnight. I might then go out to interview people concerned or attend a press conference. The rest of the day could involve anything from going to meetings to covering a court case or putting together a feature. I also write a weekly column. Most of the day is spent on the phone chasing people up for comments – anyone from council officials and MPs to owners of vegetarian dogs. I should finish at 7 p.m. but it is usually 8.30 onwards. We work nights every few weeks and work a lot of weekends.

'I enjoy the fact that no two days are the same. You're always talking to different people and it's great to feel that you know what's going on and are in a position to tell other people about it – like being first with the gossip! The downsides are the long hours – doing a full day then being asked to stay late and write an extra 700-word feature when you'd promised to meet friends in the pub. And it can be frustrating to then see that feature cut to a few lines.

'You have to be outgoing, not afraid to march up to people and chat to them, and patient when talking to people who don't want to help you. Shorthand is essential. And being able to read a map helps – I can't and am always getting lost on the way to jobs!'

Sub-editor

Sub-editors, usually known simply as subs, prepare writers' copy for publication. They ensure that a story is readable, makes sense and flows well, simplifying the complicated and weeding out clichés, jargon and gobbledygook. They will tighten up and improve a writer's copy when necessary, but a good sub has a sensitive attitude towards other people's copy and knows when to leave well alone. Subs cut copy to fit the available space, and come up with headlines, captions and introductions. They usually work to a layout supplied by the art department, but on newspapers they may design the pages themselves, deciding on the positioning of articles on the page and how to crop photos to fit the available space.

Accuracy is vital for subs and they need an eagle eye for detail. They are responsible for ensuring that grammar, punctuation and spelling are immaculate, and have to check everything with any room for error (names and places, dates of events, prices and publishers of books, etc.). Fact-checking can be tedious and sometimes difficult, but if there's a mistake, it's the subs who get the blame. They must be alert to any possible legal problems – a libel case could cost the company a lot of money and the sub her job. A sub must also ensure that all copy conforms to house style (see Chapter 9) and that the tone is suited to the publication: a piece for the *Sun* would obviously be written and subbed completely differently from one for the *Independent*.

It can be satisfying to turn rough raw copy into a polished piece of writing. However, it can also be a frustrating and often thankless task – you may do most of the work on a piece but it's the writer who gets the byline, the credit and the glory. You also need an equable temperament, a creative and original mind and a willingness to question anything you don't understand – if it doesn't make sense to you, it probably won't to the reader either. You must be able to work quickly and accurately even under extreme pressure. A good sub has an excellent general knowledge and the kind of magpie mind that collects facts, highbrow and lowbrow, whether it's being able to name the members of Blur or knowing the capital of Madagascar – or, at least, know how to find someone who can check a particular piece of information or which reference sources to use. On magazines subs generally work on copy for all areas; on a large newspaper they may be responsible for just one area, such as the sports, city or news pages.

The chief sub holds a vital – and stressful – position on any publication. She is responsible for organizing the distribution of work on the desk, organizing deadlines and taking responsibility for meeting them, liaising with the printers and managing the department. She oversees the work of the other subs, second-reading their work and rewriting headlines, introductions, etc., if necessary.

A recent NUJ survey of members' earnings found a wide spread of salaries for subs: 20 per cent earned between £25,000 and £40,000; 10 per cent earned under £15,000; 6 per cent earned over £50,000. Newspaper subs earn more than those on magazines.

Katherine Whitbourn

Age : **34**
Job : **News Sub-editor, *Daily Express***
Based : **London**
Salary range : **c. £28–45,000**
Qualifications : **MA in English; NCTJ Proficiency Certificate**

'I began as a reporter on my home town newspaper, the *Kent & Sussex Courier*, moved into subbing there, then worked on the *Western Daily Press* in Bristol and *Western Morning News* in Plymouth before coming to the *Daily Express* in 1989. I got the job by writing in on spec and travelling from Plymouth to London twice a week on my days off to do trial shifts.

'The work involves not only nights but weekends, bank holidays and Christmas Day. A working day begins at anything between 1.30 p.m. and 8 p.m. For me the biggest downside is not being able to participate in any regular weekly activity, such as a music group or sports club.

'Major plus points include being at the sharp end, knowing things before the general public does and, occasionally, knowing things they possibly never will. Immensely satisfying, also, is having something to show for every day's work. There is a terrific buzz from working on a story, then seeing it in the paper two hours later. The team spirit is fabulous and so are the laughs.

'As a sub, no experience is ever wasted – no visit to anywhere, no TV programme watched, no article skimmed. Sooner or later you will be glad you know whatever it is.

'The world of newspapers is still very male-dominated, with the exception of fashion and features. In the news production department where I work, women make up under a tenth of the staff, mostly, I suspect, because of the family-unfriendly nature of the hours. Ultimately, however, you're just a bunch of people working hard to produce a newspaper and often I have been hours into my working day before I've noticed I'm the only woman in the room. If you have a better-than-working knowledge of football, you're at a distinct advantage!

'In journalism there's no set career structure or natural progression up the ladder. You're on your own. There's no substitute for being good at the job: it doesn't guarantee success, but it helps. Remember it's a very small world, and the same people crop up again and again. Don't leave anywhere under a cloud and remember that anyone you're nasty to will one day end up in a position to be nasty to you.'

Correspondent

A correspondent contributes copy on a particular subject or geographical area. Daily papers often employ specialist correspondents, with in-depth knowledge of areas such as education, finance, social events, political news or sport. All would have excellent contacts within their field and be expected to keep in regular touch with them, encouraging them to feed in stories.

Foreign correspondents are posted to areas that generate large amounts of news. Their numbers, however, are dwindling, thanks to increasingly budget-conscious proprietors and improved technical services, such as satellites, fax machines and efficient telephone systems. Only the largest quality papers maintain permanent foreign correspondents and only in such major news centres as Washington and Tokyo. For others, it is cheaper and simple enough to send a reporter to a particular area as and when a story occurs. Many of those who work as foreign reporters do so on a freelance basis (see Stringers p. 27) or work for news agencies who supply a number of publications. You need to be an experienced reporter already (this is not a job for beginners) and to have several foreign languages under your belt – no one gets Washington as their first posting.

Janet Bush

Age : **35**
Job : **Economics Correspondent, *The Times***
Based : **London**
Salary : **£40–50,000**
Qualifications : **BA (Hons.) English Language and Literature; Postgraduate Diploma in Journalism**

'I won a financial scholarship from Reuters for the one-year postgraduate course at Cardiff. There was no guarantee of a job but after the course I did join Reuters as a trainee in London and Frankfurt, then became a reporter on their financial reporting unit. From there I went to the *Financial Times*, as deputy economics correspondent then as foreign correspondent in their New York bureau. After that I spent two years as a reporter on the BBC's *Money Programme* before joining *The Times* in 1992.

'My job involves reporting all economic news, which normally means writing every day. Stories include economic statistics, forecasts, reports, meetings of the Treasury and the Bank of England, and international economic conferences. If the Chancellor is testifying on policy to the Treasury Select Committee I would go. I also write regular features and, once a month, the main *Times* economic analysis, which highlights different economic issues in Britain or overseas.

'I travel a fair bit, going to economic conferences. Since I have been at *The Times*, I've worked in Madrid, Naples, New York, Washington, Copenhagen and Halifax, Nova Scotia. I enjoy the freedom I have to make my own judgements on what I write and considerable space and opportunity to write "think pieces". Meeting people and learning new areas is great fun. I am not a trained economist so am constantly learning. It is a great bonus to be able to ask to meet very different types of people simply because I work for a paper.

'Most useful skills include curiosity, being able to type fast, take notes accurately and not panic on deadline, keeping an open mind when pursuing a story and admitting when you don't know or understand something. Journalists are not expected to know everything but are expected to find someone who does! Be self-starting. Write articles on spec and send them to magazines or papers. Request work experience and then generate ideas. If you have a good idea, it may well be used – not least because you're cheap!

'The usefulness of contacts and "networking" cannot be over-estimated. Get to know as many people within your organization as you can. Build up contacts outside as widely as possible. Talk to everybody – everybody has something to say.'

Alexandra Duval Smith

Age : **30**
Job : **Paris Correspondent, the *Guardian* (freelance)**
Based : **Paris**
Salary : **fixed fee of £1,000 a month plus lineage (payment for commissioned articles) – total is £2,000 to £3,500 a month**
Qualifications : ***Baccalauréat* in Philosophy and Languages ('I'm half Swedish, half British and went to a French school in Stockholm')**

'The first time I had any contact with journalism was at the age of fourteen when I got the chance of being a presenter during a day devoted to children on Swedish radio. I took a liking to it and later used to skive off school, pretending I was older than I was, to work on radio programmes. At eighteen, I moved to London and was shocked to find the BBC didn't consider me experienced enough to be anchorwoman on the *Nine O'Clock News*. I quickly had to reduce my ambitions and ended up with a seemingly humdrum but incredibly useful job producing a staff newspaper for Debenhams. I was lucky, because I worked with a very experienced newspaperwoman who trained me.

'After a year I went to New York and worked wherever I could. I used to stay up until 4 a.m., buy the American papers, read them, and ring British regional papers – at 5 a.m. It was 10 a.m. in Britain and I could ring with stories before anyone else. It sounds very ambitious but it was just fun and exciting at the time. After five months I returned to the UK and spent the next five years freelance subbing and writing for everything from local papers to *Cosmo*. The more experience I gained, the more bold I became, eventually getting shifts on *Today*, *Thames News* (TV) and the *Guardian*. In 1989 I won a competition, which led to a researcher's job on *This Week*, a TV current affairs programme, for a year.

'By 1990 I'd decided the place I wanted to be was the *Guardian*, and I freelanced there in various departments before I got a staff job. After four years I left because I wanted to return to the freedom of freelancing. Then I heard about the position in Paris and two weeks later started working here. I am freelance but 90 per cent of my work is for the *Guardian*. The job is exciting because you never know what you will be doing next – chasing Eric Cantona or interviewing the French president.'

Copy Taster

A copy taster on a newspaper is responsible for assessing each story or lead as it comes in from reporters, agencies and contributors and deciding how newsworthy it is. It's a responsible job – woe betide the copy taster who spikes a story only to find all the other papers go big on it – and is therefore usually done by the desk editor or other senior journalist.

Night Editor

The night editor, a senior editorial executive on newspapers, is in charge of seeing the paper through its production cycle after the main working day is over and once basic content and form has been decided. She works shift hours along with a team of subs, journalists and designers, supervising layouts and handling of stories.

Columnist

Columnists have a regular signed column in which they write about subjects of their choice from a personal point of view. They must be opinionated and confident, and have to come up with a constant stream of subjects about which to rant passionately – not as easy as it sounds. Most columnists are experienced writers who are expected to churn out consistently interesting, relevant and topical copy, but in the case of celebrity columnists, who are employed for their pulling power rather than their writing skills, the work is often extensively rewritten or even ghosted (i.e. entirely written by someone else).

Critic

Critics review books, films, plays, records, television and radio programmes. Like columnists, they must be opinionated and tough enough to write what they feel without worrying about what others think. They should also be well informed about their subject matter, so, on the nationals at least, this is not a job for beginners. Most start by supplying reviews to a local paper or small magazine, either while on staff or as a freelance.

Stringer

Stringers are freelance journalists who feed in stories and leads from a particular area, which is cheaper for newspapers or radio/ TV stations than keeping someone permanently on staff there. They may be local newspaper reporters feeding stories to the nationals and to other media, or journalists based abroad providing reports for international media. They are usually paid per story rather than on a regular retainer so it's a tough job with no security and no guarantee of work.

Features

On newspapers, features, as distinct from news, are longer and more in-depth pieces and need not necessarily be as topical. On women's magazines, the features department is generally respons- ible for all content, apart from fashion or beauty, which can cover everything from horoscopes to film reviews, relationship advice to career quizzes.

The features editor, who may be responsible for a department of several people, decides which pieces will appear when, who will write them and how much they will be paid. Sometimes freelance writers contribute ideas, but more often they are initiated in- house, so every features editor has to come up with a constant stream of original, creative suggestions. Once ideas have been agreed, she will contact the writers and commission them: she briefs them as to what the piece is about, the angle it should take, the sorts of points it should cover, how long it should be and when it must be delivered by. This may be backed up with a written brief to confirm the details.

When the copy comes in, the features editor will read and edit it and pass it on to other senior staff for their comments. If changes are needed, she may make them herself or ask the subs to work on the copy or, if quite a bit of work is called for, rebrief the writer. Copy is usually commissioned with a specific issue in mind, but most publications try to keep a number of 'filler' items in stock to fall back on in lean times.

Most articles are commissioned from freelances though some publications employ staff feature writers, who will usually be ex- pected to be good all-rounders, able to turn their hand to anything from an in-depth health piece to a celebrity profile to a series of witty photo captions. The ability to write entertaining, educational, elegant prose, which keeps a reader enthralled from start to finish, goes without saying. Writers must also be capable of sticking to an editor's brief: if you're commissioned to do 400 words, it's no use turning in 2,000, and no one will appreciate a deeply personal opinion piece if they've asked for something practical and informative.

A features editor on a major glossy monthly would probably earn around £25–£30,000, more on a weekly or daily publication.

Michele Lavery

Age : **32**
Job : **Deputy Features Editor, *Daily Mail***
Based : **London**
Salary : **confidential**
Qualifications : **BA (Hons.) English; NCTJ sub-editing course**

'I started in journalism the day after I left university. I'd met someone at a party who worked for the editor of *Vogue*. She was desperate to move over to fashion and was asking around for anyone interested in her job. I went for an interview and didn't get that job but one on *Tatler* (owned by the same company), as editorial assistant.

'I recently moved to the *Daily Mail* from *Marie Claire*, where I was features editor for three and a half years, then assistant editor for a year. The demands of magazines and daily newspapers are quite different. A newspaper person loves the fast pace; the fact that you commission a feature by midday, by five it's written, by eight it's laid out and it's in the paper the next day. The thought of working on a feature over a period of two months fills them with horror.

'A magazine can't respond to news in the same way. *Marie Claire* works three months ahead. The skill is to anticipate which stories to avoid because they will have been all over the media by the time your magazine is out and to have ideas which will still be original.

There is much more time to discuss ideas, to edit and to work on layouts. However, the flow of work is as demanding.

'Newspaper hours are still very long in comparison with magazines. They are also inflexible. The demands of the day's news are unpredictable and you stay until the day's work is done. On magazines you have more choice about which nights or weekends you work through. Having young children and working on a daily does not combine well.

'I think it is harder to get into journalism now than it was ten years ago. It is even a struggle to get unpaid work experience. But it is experience that counts. All the qualifications and eagerness in the world are not enough. One of the most common mistakes I've seen in those applying for work experience and for jobs is to apply only to the heavyweight publications. It is worth seeking out specialist or quirky publications which may not receive so many applications.'

Denise Watson

Age : **30**
Job : **Deputy Women's Editor, *Manchester Evening News* (daily)**
Based : **Manchester**
Salary : **confidential**
Qualifications : **BA (Hons.) Politics, Thomson Certificate of Journalism**

'I started as a trainee with my local paper, the *Newcastle Chronicle*, on the Thomson Newspaper Training Scheme. I then joined the *Northern Echo* in Darlington as feature writer and sub-editor, then became feature writer on *Woman* magazine in London. In 1993 I came to the *Manchester Evening News* as feature writer and now deputy women's editor.

'The working day begins around 7.45 a.m. with a scan of the day's nationals. If there's a big story that needs a local follow-up, myself or the women's editor will deal with it immediately. I can usually find time to research and write such features for the same or next day's paper. If not, I'll commission a freelance writer instead, then arrange for a photographer to take the pictures.

'We produce an eight-page women's supplement every Wednesday, together with a daily page Monday to Saturday. It's my job to write features for each, come up with ideas for freelance writers, then help design and sub the Wednesday supplement on Apple Mac. It's non-stop work, and there's always something urgent to be done. The telephone rings constantly.

'When the women's editor is on holiday, I take on her role too. It's much the same, only she has to open the piles of post every morning, plan what will go into each weekly supplement and daily page. She does more commissioning than I do and has to deal with our advertising department more, negotiating how much space we're prepared to give up to ads – and, of course, she's responsible if anything goes wrong! On Wednesday I write a column for the main newspaper, usually something topical, giving the women's point of view. The day ends between 4 and 4.30 p.m., though sometimes I stay late if I've arranged to interview someone in the evening. By Friday I'm usually exhausted, but very proud of what we've achieved – and feel justified in nipping out for a quick glass of wine at lunchtime.

'The perks and benefits are brilliant. As well as being paid very well, we get seven weeks' holiday a year, free health insurance, a car allowance payment and time off in lieu if we work a lot of overtime. We also get travel press trips and free samples from cosmetics PRs.'

Commissioning Editor

Commissioning editors are responsible for commissioning copy from writers. As well as being used as a job title in its own right, 'commissioning editor' is also a general term for anyone who commissions, though they may be called deputy features editor, health editor, etc. They would probably earn in the region of £25–30,000.

Contributing Editor

This is the term used for a freelance journalist who works from home rather than at the office but has a contract with a publication. This dictates the number of pieces they're expected to contribute each year and usually restricts them from writing for other competing titles. In return, they may be paid a regular retainer fee or at a slightly higher rate per article than normal.

Fashion and Beauty Editors

Women's magazines are heavily dependent on advertising from the large cosmetic, perfume and fashion companies. The fashion and beauty editors are therefore senior members of staff, whose roles call for good diplomacy and PR skills and require them to attend a large number of receptions and launches.

As well as writing copy on their subject area, fashion and beauty editors also spend quite a bit of time out of the office, overseeing photographic sessions ('shoots'). Much of their time in the office is spent organizing the next shoot and seeing the constant stream of models, hair and make-up artists and photographers who come in to show their books (photographic portfolios of previous work).

When a fashion or beauty editor has decided on a story to do, she or her assistant will start ringing round designers and cosmetic companies asking if they have anything that fits the brief and calling in clothes and samples. Once these are all in, the editor selects the items she wants for her story and decides which models, hair and make-up artists, and photographer to use. The assistant will then book studios and people, or put an option on them, to be confirmed at a later date. If the story is to be shot abroad, the assistant has the long and boring, but unavoidable, task of preparing a carnet for foreign customs: this is a comprehensive list of every item of clothing, accessories etc. being taken on the shoot and how much each is worth. As budgets are usually limited, foreign shoots generally mean extensive negotiations with airlines, hotels and tourist offices to try to get free or discounted flights and rooms in return for mentions in the magazine.

On the shoot, an assistant will find herself doing everything from carrying luggage to unpacking and ironing clothes, and generally being a slave. The editor, who is there to oversee the shoot and make sure she gets the sort of pictures she wants, may also have to muck in. Once a shoot is over the fashion department has to pack everything up and send it back to the designers; beauty departments rarely have to return samples.

Jobs in fashion and beauty can involve working with temperamental characters, so you have to be friendly and easygoing (and able to hold your tongue!). It goes without saying that you should be passionately interested in fashion or beauty, too. Beauty journalists are expected to be able to write; many fashion journalists can get by on visual flair and original ideas, but if they can combine that with great writing skills, they'll be hugely in demand. All fashion and beauty staff must have a clear understanding of their readership – it's no use featuring designer fashions and expensive cosmetics in a magazine bought by people whose budget only stretches to C&A or Boots' own brand. These are the best departments to work in if it's freebies you're after – despite the recession, fashion and cosmetics companies are still pretty generous with their gifts and discounts!

A fashion or beauty editor on a glosssy magazine would probably earn around £30,000; a junior assistant in the same department is likely to earn in the region of £10–11,000.

Angela Buttolph

Age : **24**
Job : **Merchandise editor, *Elle* (monthly)**
Based : **London**
Salary : **confidential**
Qualifications : **BTEC National Diploma in Business and Finance;**
BTEC HND in Business of Fashion Management

'My first job was with a clothing company, modelling for buyers, delivering samples and doing general admin. I then went to college and during the course had to do work placements in an administration department. I wrote to high-profile companies and they all said I was the first person to ask for work experience in admin, rather than fashion or features, so I got lots of offers, including *Elle*. After my placement here I stayed in contact – and when a job came up as their receptionist they remembered me.

'I did that for just over a year, answering telephones and doing general admin, hoping to get a job in the fashion department. No positions were available, though, so I went to the London College of Fashion to do an HND. I kept in contact with friends on *Elle* and when someone from the fashion department handed in her notice she called to let me know there would be a vacancy.

'It's a very exciting environment to work in and everyone is fairly young, which is fun. No one on fashion magazines seems to earn much money – the idea is that the prestige and the perks should make up for it, which is probably true to a certain extent. We do get loads of perks – discount cards, tickets for the London shows, occasional film screenings, endless launch parties and free issues of *Elle*!

'As merchandise editor, I compile the credits for the fashion pages and the stockists page, finding prices and fabrics for all the clothes featured. It is a very straightforward administrative job and I spend all day on the telephone to PRs. I also deal with readers' shopping queries and general admin for the fashion department.

The thing I enjoy most is writing, which isn't, strictly speaking, part of my job so I've had to do it off my own bat. I find it very challenging, partly because I haven't had any training.

'It's important to be enthusiastic – a magazine is very much a team effort so everyone needs to do their bit – and to be pleasant to people. It's such a stressful environment that anyone who can keep their cool under pressure and remain cheerful stands out.'

Liz Silvester

Age : **33**
Job : **Beauty Editor, *Essentials* (monthly)**
Based : **London**
Salary : **£23,000**
Qualifications : **7 O levels; 2 A levels**

'After A levels I went into a full-time version of my Saturday job, selling cosmetics in West End stores and branches of Boots. This gave me huge insight into the world of cosmetics and toiletries but after three years I'd had enough and did a year's secretarial course. I joined *Mizz* magazine in 1984 as editorial secretary and was very lucky as I was encouraged to get involved in all aspects of the magazine and, because of my background, was given the beauty Q&A pages to do. From there I went to be editorial/fashion assistant on *Wedding and Home*, beauty editor on *Just 17*, then deputy beauty editor on *Woman's Own*. Going from being on my own to a department of four on a mass-market weekly was really good experience. I became beauty editor on *Essentials* in 1989.

'The best bit about the job is that no two days are alike. I could be doing some or all of the following: thinking up beauty ideas for future issues and discussing them with the editor; writing copy; liaising with the editor and art editor over how features are going to look on the page; organizing and directing photographic shoots; ploughing through mountains of press releases, trying to find relevant information; answering readers' letters and phone inquiries; going out to see PRs to find out about new products; meeting promotions people to discuss beauty promotion ideas . . . I have to work to budgets on a daily basis so, as well as a writer and stylist, I have to be a mathematician and accountant too!

'I'm a make-up junkie so I love all the freebie products that land on my desk. There are so many, it's almost obscene, plus lots of nice excursions when companies are launching a new product. Two or three times a year I do a shoot abroad (usually Miami). The organization that goes into it is horrendous, sorting out your budget, booking tickets and hotels, negotiating fees, etc. – all on top of your usual day's work when really you need a week to concentrate on just that. But then you get to spend a week somewhere hot and sunny when London's cold and blustery, usually with a great team of people.'

Practicals

'Practicals' is the word used to describe home-interest features: cookery, decorating, handicrafts, etc. They may be the responsibility of a practicals editor or, on a magazine where they play only a small part, overseen by the features editor. Most people working in practicals are first and foremost specialists in their subject rather than journalists, and knowledge and experience of the relevant field is considered more important than writing ability. Cookery editors, for example, are usually trained home economists who can devise inspirational and workable recipes; a homes editor is employed primarily for her great visual flair and creative ideas. The writing can always be sorted out in-house.

Production Editor

The production editor makes sure that the publication is printed, on time and to budget, and oversees the quality of printing, paper and related costs. She has to ensure that copy gets to the printers and through the system at the right time, so must be willing to chase journalists whose copy is late, and to crack the whip over the art and subs departments. She is responsible for co-ordinating editorial and advertisements and liaises between editorial staff, typesetters and printers. She therefore has to be tremendously organized and must have a clear and logical mind. Since the advent of new technology, the role of production editor is now often divided up between members of the sub-editing team, or may have become part of the managing editor's job.

A production editor on a trade title might earn around £19–24,000; on a bigger title more like £25–30,000.

Secretaries/Assistants

Starting out in a secretarial role is an excellent way to find out exactly what's going on, how the whole publication works and what the readers really think – readers are constantly calling newspapers and magazines on a million and one different subjects and a secretary will often have far more day-to-day contact with the people buying the magazine than an editor does.

As a secretary or assistant, you may be responsible for paying contributors, chasing outstanding copy, opening and sifting post, inputting copy from freelances (if they don't send in disks), keeping a desk diary, answering readers' queries, maintaining files, providing a support service to journalists, etc. Like everybody else on the staff, you'll have to work to tight deadlines. You'll need all the usual skills, including fast, impeccable typing, computer literacy, organizational ability, good communications skills and a great telephone manner.

Starting salaries for junior assistants/secretaries would generally be between £10,000 and £15,000.

Caitlin Bodrugan

Age : **27**
Job : **Editorial assistant, *Earth Matters*/PA to Head of Publications and Information, Friends of the Earth**
Based : **London**
Salary range : **£14,500–16,500**
Qualifications : **B.Sc. (Hons.) natural sciences**

'After university, I went on an environmental expedition to Tanzania for three months. Back in England, I temped as a receptionist for a few months, then worked at the Science Museum as an "explainer". My next job was as PA to the MD of a small firm, running the administrative side of the business. I then left London and spent over a year in Cornwall, unemployed – a blow to the ego and very demoralizing. I returned to London in 1992 and did some unpaid work for an MP from Cornwall, writing press releases and administering a fund-raising scheme. Voluntary work saved my self-confidence and reinspired me.

'In March 1993, after applying unsuccessfully for a job at Friends of the Earth, I started volunteering in their publications and information department. I took a temporary contract that summer as PA to the head of department, followed by a temporary admin job in the fund-raising department. When the PA post came up again on a permanent basis, I applied for and was offered it.

'My job includes many editorial functions. As well as working on *Earth Matters*, FOEs quarterly magazine which my boss edits, I compile and edit a monthly newsletter for over 250 local groups. The work ranges from keeping the diary, faxing and photocopying to copy-chasing, laying out a newsletter, liaising with contributors and printers, and answering readers' queries. I regularly get involved in demonstrations and actions, from filling in the outline of a seventy-foot chalk figure of John Major in his underpants as part of a protest against road-building, to getting wrapped up in paper to deliver a petition against overpackaging to the Environment Minister.

'I proofread nearly all FOE publications, from the kids' leaflets and posters to the academic reports and Bills to be put before Parliament. That means I get to read some of the most up-to-date research on a whole range of environmental issues, which makes me feel well informed and positive about the work.

'The best thing is working with a dedicated and fun bunch of people for an organization at the forefront of the environmental movement and knowing that you have the power to change things for the better.'

Getting into Newspapers and Magazines

The traditional route into newspapers, known as 'direct entry', is to join a local newspaper and undergo the apprenticeship-style training provided by the industry's training organization, the National Council for the Training of Journalists (NCTJ). This would once have been mainly for school and college-leavers but is now increasingly dominated by graduates – a recent survey found that graduates accounted for 68 per cent of journalism trainees on regional and local papers.

Would-be direct entrants need to apply to the editor of the paper for employment as a trainee. If you can show you've already started to learn shorthand and typing, or had work published, so much the better. Direct entrants working towards NCTJ qualifications undertake a mix of distance learning, on-the-job training and block-release courses. All trainees must pass qualifying exams in subjects including law, public administration and newspaper journalism and achieve 100 w.p.m. shorthand. They then have to serve with a newspaper for eighteen months to two years, at the end of which they can sit for the National Certificate (eventually to be replaced by an NVQ or SVQ Level 4). Contact the NCTJ direct for more details (see Chapter 10).

Others come into the industry after attending a full-time

vocational training course (usually one year minimum), many of which are for graduates only. This is the increasingly popular 'pre-entry' route. In the case of pre-entry students on an NCTJ-approved course, the preliminary exams are taken while at college; like direct entrants, they then serve a period of work experience before sitting for the National Certificate. It is also possible to take two-to three-year HND or degree courses. Chapter 9 includes details of these and pre-entry courses.

Some newspaper groups run their own in-house training schemes, including the Croydon Advertiser Group, Westminster Press, Trinity International Holdings, EMAP, Eastern Counties Newspapers, Argus Newspapers, Southern Newspapers, and Midland News Association (see Chapter 11 for contact addresses).

As in all areas of the media, jobs on national papers are rarely advertised: people are recruited via word of mouth, or sometimes start by working freelance shifts.

Various national papers offer places to graduate trainees but competition for these is extremely fierce as there are usually only two or three places a year on each scheme, for which thousands apply. They include the *Daily Express*, *The Times*, the *Sunday Times*, the *Financial Times* and Mirror Group Newspapers. You'll need to keep an eye out in the national and trade press for advertisements, or write to the personnel director of the relevant paper for details (see Chapter 11 for addresses).

Reuters also run high-calibre graduate-training schemes each year. These last two and a half years and the minimum entry requirement is a second class honours degree. You should also have a proven interest in current affairs and be fluent in at least one language, apart from English. Between five and six hundred apply each year for the ten places on the graduate scheme. For details, contact Graduate Recruitment, Reuters Limited, 85 Fleet Street, London EC4P 4AJ.

Entry to magazine journalism is less formal and structured than to newspaper journalism. Although those starting out in magazines are more likely than entrants to newspaper journalism to be graduates (over 85 per cent, according to the PPA), they are less likely to have had professional journalism training. However, openings are few and far between. You greatly increase your chances if you concentrate on finding something on a trade or special-interest title rather than pinning your hopes on high-profile magazines where competition for entry-level jobs is incredibly fierce. Wherever you start, though, you'll have to begin at the bottom and work your way up. However good you think you are, no one will want to take you on as a writer or editor until you have some experience behind you.

When it comes to finding a journalistic job, it helps to be in the right place at the right time. Most publications look at their own staff before employing an unknown quantity from outside, so no would-be editor should turn up her nose at menial jobs or the chance to do a few weeks' work experience. Once you have a foot in the door it is much easier to convince your superiors of your talent. Don't ignore the secretarial route: it may be much maligned but magazines are more open than some other branches of the media to people starting as secretaries and working their way up. Many brilliant writers and editors started their careers this way.

Another way to make the break into writing is to enter competitions and awards run by newspapers and magazines. You can find details of some in the *Writers' & Artists' Yearbook* and *The Writers' Handbook* (see Chapter 15). Winners and runners-up usually see their pieces appear in print and get the chance to make contacts and suggest more ideas.

There are few formal trainee schemes in magazine publishing and many were a casualty of the recession, but it's hoped they may restart as things pick up. Among those companies who take on trainees are IPC Magazines and Reed Business Publishing. Some accept a minimum of two A levels as qualification; others prefer you to have already completed some kind of journalistic training. You'll find contact addresses for the main magazine publishers in Chapter 11.

Chapter 3 / **Radio and Television**

Like other areas of the media, broadcasting is a fast-moving and ever-evolving world. Just how quickly things have changed in this relatively young industry is obvious when you think that our first TV channel, BBC1, went on air only sixty years ago, in 1936, and had the screen to itself for nearly twenty years until it was joined in 1955 by ITV, in 1964 by BBC2 and in 1982 by Channel 4, with satellite and cable following a few years later. BBC radio arrived in the 1920s and its local radio stations in 1967 (the same year colour TV was launched). From just two commercial radio stations in 1973 we now have around 200. The first national independent radio stations were launched as recently as 1992.

And the changes show no sign of slowing down. We're just about to gain another terrestrial TV station, with the launch of Channel 5 in 1997. Another radio waveband, Digital Audio Broadcasting (DAB), is expected to come on air in 1996, providing a new high-quality transmission system. In the next ten to fifteen years, advances in broadcasting, computing and telecommunications technology will continue to have a radical effect on both production and transmission of programmes. We'll see the arrival of high-definition widescreen TV pictures and cinema-quality images, with interference-free CD-quality stereo sound on radio and TV. There will be interactive home shopping, home banking, training and information services. Viewers will be able to choose what to watch and when and, just as there are specialist trade publications, specialized TV channels will be aimed at specific groups such as doctors or teachers. New digital technology promises an explosion of both TV and radio stations to come in the near future.

This should mean more jobs for journalists – although not

necessarily in great numbers. The rapid developments in technology mean that, as in other industries, machines can now do many jobs that used to need people. They have also led to the growth of what is known as 'multi-skilling': people are now called upon to perform a range of tasks, whereas they might once have specialized. For example, one big advance has been in the use of video, which is both cheaper and faster than film and requires less bulky equipment and fewer people to operate it. As a result, instead of going on a story accompanied by camera and sound technicians, a reporter may now be responsible for doing her own filming and sound-recording as well as reporting.

There has also been a growth in 'bi-media' working, whereby reporters and specialist correspondents produce stories for both radio and TV. This is largely confined to the BBC at the moment but may increase as independent TV and radio stations in the same region team up to pool resources. There are obvious benefits for the employer, but an NUJ survey claimed that bi-media working was resulting in longer working hours, more stress and low morale.

In this book we are dealing only with those jobs which use journalistic skills, but the vast majority of jobs in broadcasting are on the technical and craft side: there are masses of opportunities from camera operators to casting directors, set designers to dressmakers, lighting technicians to make-up artists. The range of programmes you could work on is huge, too, with both TV and radio covering every conceivable subject area from news and current affairs to drama, religion to sports. In each area, the basic job descriptions are the same but they may call for different interests or areas of knowledge. A producer of natural-history programmes may have a degree in zoology, for example, while politics or economics would be more relevant for someone working in current affairs.

The broadcast media's great advantage over other media is their topicality. They don't have to wait till the next day to tell a story but can relay it straight away, and even follow it as it happens. Radio, with no cameras and lighting to worry about, can respond particularly quickly, as can services such as Teletext and Ceefax, where a story can be on air in the time it takes to type it.

Like other media industries, broadcasting is very much London-heavy but there *are* jobs on local TV and radio stations around the country. Salaries, however, are higher on national stations, and higher in TV than in radio.

Working in broadcasting certainly has a glamorous image and it can be both exciting and satisfying to work in an area which plays an important role in so many people's lives. In a typical week, for example, 94 per cent of the population watches television. You may also be pleased to hear that the industry has a relatively youthful workforce: a Skillset survey into employment trends in the radio industry found that the average age was thirty-three. However, as mentioned in the Introduction, it is an insecure area in which to work. Both the BBC and the ITV companies have cut back the number of permanent staff in recent years and now use lots of freelances brought in on short-term contracts.

BBC

The BBC is the giant of British broadcasting. It operates two national terrestrial TV networks (BBC1 and BBC2), a satellite TV channel (BBC World), five national radio networks (Radios 1, 2, 3, 4 and 5 Live), forty local radio stations in England and others in Scotland, Wales and Northern Ireland. The Foreign Office-funded BBC World Service provides programmes in thirty-nine different languages to 120 million listeners around the world.

In addition, BBC Worldwide Publishing (producing programme-related books, magazines and videos, audio tapes) and BBC Worldwide Television (responsible for exporting programmes and developing new satellite and cable channels) work to generate as much income as possible to supplement the licence fee. There is also a vast range of back-up departments, including libraries, news information services (who can do research and provide cuttings) and a pronunciations unit. The BBC Monitoring Service in

Reading listens to radio and TV broadcasts from around the world and provides news and information from the world's media to the Government, BBC journalists and commercial and media customers.

The BBC is divided into six regions: three national (BBC Scotland, BBC Wales and BBC Northern Ireland) and three within England (BBC North, BBC Midlands and East, and BBC South). The Corporation has a policy of establishing 'centres of excellence' in the regions: Manchester is the base of religion, sport and youth programmes; Pebble Mill in Birmingham specializes in daytime/leisure programming and drama; and Bristol is the home of natural history, documentaries and features. Around a quarter of the BBC's staff are employed outside London and the Corporation is aiming to increase the proportion of programmes made outside the capital.

In all, the BBC employs around 22,000 people. News and Current Affairs is one of the biggest departments, accounting for more than 1,700 staff across both TV and radio.

ITV Network

ITV is the overall term for the regional companies that make up the national independent television network. Each pays an annual licence fee to the Treasury. The current fifteen regional ITV licensees (whose franchises run for a ten-year period from 1 January 1993) are: Anglia Television (East of England); Border Television (Borders and the Isle of Man); Carlton Broadcasting (London region, weekdays); Central Broadcasting (East, West and South Midlands); Channel Television (the Channel Islands); Grampian Television (North of Scotland); Granada Television (North-west England); HTV Group (Wales and West of England); LWT (London region, weekends); Meridian Broadcasting (South and South-east England); Scottish Television (Central Scotland); Tyne Tees Television (North-east England); Ulster Television (Northern Ireland); Westcountry Television (South-west England); Yorkshire

Television (Yorkshire). In addition, GMTV provides a national breakfast-time service for the third channel.

The independent companies' income is derived from selling airtime to advertisers. The bigger the audience they can deliver to advertisers, the higher their income, hence ITV's emphasis on popular programming. Commercial sponsorship of programmes is also allowed, although it is strictly controlled (there can be no sponsorship of news and current affairs programmes, for example).

Some companies produce their own programmes and may be renowned for certain areas. Anglia, for example, produces the much-respected *Survival* natural history series; Granada has a reputation for big dramas such as *Brideshead Revisited*, *Jewel in the Crown*, and also, of course, for *Coronation Street*. Other companies, like Carlton, are 'publisher broadcasters' or 'publisher/contractors', who commission most of their work from independent production companies and consequently have smaller staffs. Granada is the largest company, with around 1,600 employees; Channel, the smallest, has a staff of only around 120.

At the centre of the ITV structure is ITV Network Centre in London, which acts as a collective commissioner and scheduler of programmes for the network. Programmes may be commissioned from independent production companies or from those regional companies that have their own production facilities. The regional companies submit everything, including ads, to the Centre for approval.

ITN

Independent Television News, which went on air in 1955, is the independent organization currently authorized by the ITC (Independent Television Commission) to provide national and international news coverage across the ITV network and Channel 4. (Local news and magazine programmes for each ITV region are produced by journalists working in the relevant regional company.) Based in London, ITN employs just under 600 people, around a third of whom are journalists.

Channel 4

The newest terrestrial channel, networked throughout the UK apart from Wales, started broadcasting in November 1982 with a remit to cater for minority audiences whose needs were rarely met by the other channels. The launch of Channel 4 provided a huge boost for independent production companies as all but one of its programmes are commissioned from other organizations (ITV companies or independent producers). The only programme to be produced in-house is *Right to Reply*, which maintains a small research department.

S4C

Sianel Pedwar Cymru, based in Cardiff, is the Welsh fourth channel, providing programmes in both English and Welsh. It doesn't produce any programmes itself: the English-language output comes from Channel 4, while Welsh programmes are provided by HTV, the BBC and independent producers.

Satellite and Cable

Around eighty television channels are available on satellite and cable in the UK, funded by a mix of subscription fees from viewers and advertising revenue. Around 4.5 million homes in Britain currently subscribe to cable and satellite services, a number which is expected to rise to around 10 million within five years. Many of the stations specialize in a certain genre, such as film, sport, travel, music or light entertainment. Unlike the terrestrial channels, cable and satellite channels are not obliged to carry a mix of information, education and entertainment, but they must adhere to the ITC's Codes on Programmes, Advertising and Sponsorship.

The twenty-four-hour news channels employ journalists but many of the other stations buy in most of their programming rather than originating it. One exception is BSkyB, the main satellite company in Britain, with nine channels (Sky News, Sky Sports, Sky Movies, etc.) and a stake in Nickelodeon, the children's channel and QVC, the home-shopping channel.

Cable is a means of distribution not only for cable-exclusive channels like the Travel Channel and the Parliamentary Channel, but also for Astra satellite channels, terrestrial television services, telephone communications and radio stations such as Sky Radio and Radio Luxembourg. It will also make local broadcasting more widely available in future, which may eventually provide a useful way for beginners to gain hands-on television experience.

Independent Production Companies

In Britain and Europe, broadcasting is moving away from large organizations and towards smaller independent production companies, known in the industry simply as 'independents'. They were given a huge boost by the launch of Channel 4 in 1982, followed by the requirement of the 1990 Broadcasting Act that both BBC and ITV take 25 per cent of their non-news and current affairs output from independents.

There are now over 1,000 independent production companies in the UK producing TV and radio programmes, pop videos, commercials and training films. You'll find many of the main ones listed in *The Writers' Handbook* or *Broadcast Production Guide*. Some specialize in a particular field – comedy, for example, or food and gardening programmes. They may produce a whole series or contribute individual programmes within a strand. A few companies are large enough to keep permanent staff but most are small, with a core staff supplemented by freelance workers on short-term contracts as and when they are needed.

Text Services: Teletext/Ceefax

Electronic text services are broadcast pages of text that can be received on television sets with the requisite decoder, which most sets now have. Updated constantly throughout the day, they relay national, international and regional news and information on everything from the weather to travel conditions, TV listings to sports results. The two main services are Teletext, which appears on ITV and Channel 4 and is fed by the Press Association, and Ceefax, shown on BBC1 and BBC2 and produced by the BBC's News and Current Affairs Directorate. Another service, Prestel, is operated by British Telecom for paying subscribers. Text services may employ both writers and subs.

Independent Radio

The first commercial radio stations were LBC, now defunct, and Capital in 1973 and there are now over 150 in the Independent Local Radio (ILR) network. Licences to broadcast are granted on a competitive franchise basis by the Radio Authority, which also oversees stations' output. More licences will become available in early 1996, with the opening up of new FM radio frequencies.

As well as the local commercial stations, the 1990 Broadcasting Act gave the go-ahead for three national commercial radio stations. The first Independent National Radio station to broadcast was Classic FM, in September 1992, followed in April 1993 by Virgin 1215 and, in early 1995, by Talk Radio UK. Another relatively recent development was the launch, in autumn 1994, of five regional ILR stations: Century Radio (in the North-east), Galaxy Radio (Severn Estuary), Heart FM (Midlands/London), Jazz FM 100.4/102.2 (North-west/London) and Scot FM (Central Scotland). More are planned for the near future.

Broadcast News Services

Just as national and local papers subscribe to wire services, so commercial TV and radio stations employ agencies, such as IRN, Network News and Reuters TV and Radio News, to provide them with a news service. For radio news, this may come either in the form of complete bulletins or in component elements that can be mixed with local material by the individual stations. As well as general news, they can also supply specialized news in areas such as entertainment, sports and finance.

Miscellaneous Radio

Broadcasters outside the UK

Some English-language radio stations based outside the UK can be heard here: Atlantic 252, for example, is broadcast from Eire but reaches about two-thirds of the UK. Further afield, there are English-language services from Ghana to Guyana, Brunei to Belize. Each year the Commonwealth Broadcasting Association publishes *Who's Who in Commonwealth Broadcasting*, containing details of English-speaking TV and radio stations.

RSLs (Restricted Service Licences)

These are temporary low-powered radio stations, usually set up for four weeks at a time but occasionally for longer, perhaps linked to some big local event or sometimes as a trial run for people hoping to demonstrate the local need for a particular type of radio station. They provide a valuable way for beginners to acquire live broadcasting experience. Licences are issued by the Radio Authority, who also provide guidance notes for applicants.

In-house Radio Stations

A number of shops, including Asda, Top Shop and Texas, have their own radio stations. Other organizations are in on the act too: Blackpool Pleasure Beach, for instance, has one – Kit Kat Radio. The boom in air travel has also meant a rise in the number of in-flight radio services.

Student Radio

There are around twenty-five campus radio stations in Britain, staffed by volunteers and funded by grants from student unions. They are run on a shoestring but can be a useful way to acquire hands-on broadcasting experience.

Hospital Radio

There are over 320 hospital broadcasting stations, providing local radio programmes to 90 per cent of hospital patients in over 800 hospitals in the UK. The stations, staffed totally by unpaid volunteers – over 11,000 of them – carry no ads and are funded by money raised in the community. They range in size and scope: the smallest has just four members, the largest 100; some broadcast all day; others may be on air for only a few hours in the evening. They provide a mix of advice and entertainment, playing patients' requests, local news, interviews, sports, radio bingo, etc.

Community Radio

Community radio stations developed in the early 1980s. They are locally owned and controlled and aim to meet the needs of local areas or communities of interest, providing them with access to training, production and transmission facilities. In 1995 there were about ten community radio stations with permanent licences in the UK. They are heavily dependent on volunteers and act as a gateway into mainstream broadcasting. This is a particularly young field, with over half the workforce aged between 15 and 29.

Services Broadcasting

SSVC (Services Sound and Vision Corporation) is funded by the Ministry of Defence to provide armed forces at home and abroad with entertainment and training via its two broadcasting divisions, SSVC Television and BFBS (British Forces Broadcasting Service) radio, both based in the south-east and staffed largely by civilians. SSVC Television relies mostly on bought-in programmes; BFBS originates most of its programming.

The Job Descriptions

Generally, the skills you need as a journalist in broadcasting are common to both radio and television, especially in news and current affairs where jobs are now often bi-media. Exact job titles and duties vary from company to company and even from programme to programme but the following descriptions will give you an idea of the most common responsibilities in each.

News Reporter

In many respects, a broadcast reporter's work is similar to that of a newspaper journalist, but one major difference is that the TV or radio reporter has to think not about how the story reads on paper but about how it *sounds*. Copy must be punchier and contractions such as 'don't' and 'he'll', which are sometimes frowned on in print, are often preferred on air to 'do not' and 'he will' because they sound more natural. In broadcast news, you also have to get the point across clearly and immediately – a newspaper reader can reread a confusing paragraph but a TV viewer or radio listener can't ask a news presenter to repeat herself. On most popular radio stations, a bulletin will probably be around three to five minutes in total, with each item usually only twenty to thirty seconds long; a reporter must be able to condense the most important points of the story into an exact given time. It takes longer to speak words than to read them, so you may have only around 100 words a minute to play with. In television, this is greatly helped by visual aids – it may be a cliché but it is true that a picture can be worth a thousand words.

Once the reporters have been assigned their stories, they may spend time in the office setting things up and finding people to talk to, or go straight out on location. Depending on the story, a reporter might be accompanied by a crew of camera, sound and lighting technicians, or may go with just one other person to do both sound and pictures. In some cases, it may even be the reporter doing the whole thing. The reporter and camera operator between them work out the best shots to take; the reporter also has to find out exactly what's going on, discover the key people to talk to and decide how best to report the story.

It is vital in this job to be able to get on with all sorts of people, from a self-publicizing politician to the parents of a murdered child, to persuade them to talk about their experiences. You need the confidence to ask awkward questions, the social skills to ask them in an acceptable way and the tact to be able to drag people back to the point when they drift off at a tangent.

Live reporting and interviewing is particularly demanding. There's no time to polish up your performance, so you have to be able to think on your feet, taking in and understanding information instantly and conveying it in a clear form to the audience. It takes skill to phrase things correctly off the top of your head, without the benefits of retakes or editing.

Adaptability is important: a reporter may need to switch rapidly from one story to another, or cover the same story for different bulletins or programmes and have to adapt her approach as necessary. She must keep up to date with running stories by listening to other stations and reading newspapers and be well informed about current affairs, so that if she's sent out on a rush job with no time to research she won't be totally at sea. At the end of the day, her story may be dropped if something more important crops up, so she must be able to cope with rejection.

The radio reporter needs a blend of journalistic skills and the ability to operate technical equipment, to record stories or edit tape. She must pay even more attention to how things *sound*, and just as television news programmes look for eye-catching images to accompany a story, so radio reporters try to capture colourful noise. One of the advantages of radio reporting, though, is the speed with which it can be carried out: while TV crews have to set up lights and camera, the radio reporter can just get straight in there with her mike.

Broadcast news is a highly pressurized area, whatever your job or level of seniority. It involves working to extremely short and strict deadlines, often live, and, given the nature of news, there is little time to prepare and turn round items. Everything must be as fresh and up-to-the-minute as possible, so stories may be changed seconds before they go on air. Time is always short.

A regional radio reporter would earn between £13,000 and £22,000. Salaries on national stations and in television are higher.

Angela Johnston

Age : **25**
Job : **Junior journalist, Century Radio**
Based : **Gateshead**
Salary : **c. £13,000**
Qualifications : **BA (Hons.) Classics; Postgraduate Diploma in Radio Journalism**

'I left London University and had no idea what to do, but I'd been editor of the college newspaper and involved with hospital radio so I came up with radio journalism and did a postgrad diploma at Sunderland University, which offered work on a local community radio station, Wear FM. When I left I answered an ad in the *Guardian* for a trainee journalist at Century Radio, a new regional station, and started work there three months before its launch in September 1994. Three hundred people had applied for the job.

'There are three shifts I work from week to week: early shift (5 a.m. to 2 p.m.), day shift (9 a.m. to 7 p.m.) and late shift (11 a.m. to 9 p.m.). A typical day depends on what shift I'm doing, but usually it means finding out the main stories of the day; going out to interview people; calling police, fire and ambulance controls; doing telephone interviews; reading news; and preparing scripts for the two-hour news programme from 5 p.m. to 7 p.m.

'What I enjoy most about my work is doing something different each day and meeting lots of people from various backgrounds. I enjoy the challenge of some stories, the ones that always seem impossible, and it's brilliant if you get a new angle or an "exclusive". Being the only journalist to get someone to talk is a wonderful feeling and delights the rest of the newsroom too.

'The downsides are what we call "death knocks". Say someone's child is murdered, then I would be sent out to the police press conference, then have to try and get the child's parents to talk to me. It's not easy knowing you're upsetting someone who's going through hell. You never get used to it.

'You have to be determined but patient. Working as part of a team is vital – there's no room for prima donnas. And you have to be prepared to work hard: it's not a nine-to-five day, it's a way of life and you have to be committed to it. Often I get fed up with the long hours and the low pay but I love the job so it's worth sticking at.'

Correspondent

A correspondent is a reporter who specializes in a particular area where detailed knowledge is called for, for example, in health, economic affairs, politics, arts. As mentioned earlier, there is a growing trend, especially in the BBC, for bi-media correspondents, who produce work for both TV and radio.

A foreign correspondent may be permanently stationed in a major capital, such as Washington, Tokyo or Moscow, or sent out as and when a big news story breaks abroad, such as in Bosnia or the Gulf. They may have to work in dangerous conditions so are usually trained in health and safety techniques and equipped with flak jackets and helmets. The world's largest network of foreign correspondents is that of the BBC but, in general, numbers have decreased as companies cut back on costs by using the services of a news-agency reporter or freelances already on the scene.

News Presenter

News presenters (also referred to as newsreaders, newscasters and anchors) are the public face of broadcast news. Studio-based, they act as the central link, pulling the various strands together. They introduce the different news items, usually reading from a pre-prepared script on a prompter, though they would also have a script on the desk in case the prompter fails. Some write the script themselves and may even research it; others have it prepared for them but may rewrite it to suit their individual style of delivery.

There's more to the job than having an attractive face and a clear voice, and most news presenters are experienced journalists who've served their time as reporters in TV, radio or newspapers. Just like reporters, they have to be constantly up to date with the news and aware of breaking stories, so that they can cope with live interviews and won't be caught unprepared by any sudden programme changes.

News programmes are, naturally, live so there's plenty of scope for things to go wrong and a presenter must be quick on her feet. Reports and interviews may fail to appear on cue and she will have to improvise or rearrange the order of the items. Last-minute news may come in for which no rehearsal or preparation is possible. Throughout the broadcast, the programme director relays instructions to a TV newsreader through an earpiece, yet she still has to talk normally and calmly. Part of the skill is to make it all look and sound so much easier than it is. In radio, presenters may also operate the studio controls.

A presenter must be able to read scripts without stumbling over words (foreign names can be especially tricky) – if she pronounces things incorrectly, it damages her credibility and that of the station. She also needs to time her delivery to fit in with the programme length and time signals coming from the control room. She must ensure she doesn't let any personal prejudice show through – broadcasters have a legal obligation to be impartial, unlike newspapers, which are free to proclaim their political loyalties. A radio newsreader must compensate for the lack of a visual element by making sure her voice is full of expression. All presenters have to be consistently on form, even if they've had a heavy night the night before or whatever personal traumas they may be going through.

A news presenter on local radio would probably earn between £16,000 and £24,000. Salaries are higher in national TV and radio.

Editor

An editor determines the style and content of a programme. She may be in charge of a specific programme or, in a series or strand, responsible for the whole operation. In radio, an editor might be responsible for four of five different programmes, with a producer on each looking to her for guidance and ultimate editorial authority. Precise tasks vary from editor to editor, but generally the role is managerial and might encompass such aspects as planning, handling budgets, managing staff and taking the final decision on programme content.

In news and current affairs the news editor decides which stories to include in a bulletin and which to ignore, how long to give them and where to place them in the running order, that is, the order of priority. Every day she chairs the newsroom's morning conference to discuss stories, leads and ideas. Before getting in to work, the team will have scanned the papers and listened to news bulletins to catch up with what's going on and check for stories to follow up. There will be planned events and conferences in the diary for that day. Once the news editor knows what she's got to choose from, she assigns reporters to stories and has to keep tabs on who's chasing what and what resources are allocated where. She also considers how to use graphics or video clips to bring stories alive.

Throughout the day, regular meetings will be held to update the situation for each bulletin. As well as working on today's stories, the editor will also be noting those to be followed up the next day. Depending on the size of the programme, there may be a deputy or managing editor, also at senior level, and perhaps a home editor and foreign editor responsible for co-ordinating domestic and international news. In a small regional newsroom, one person might fill the role.

Sara Nathan

Age : **39**
Job : **Editor, *Channel Four News***
Based : **London**
Salary : **'more than I expected'**
Qualifications : **BA (Cantab.) History**

'I worked at the BBC for fifteen years, starting out on the news trainee scheme and then working on a number of news and current affairs programmes, both TV and radio, before moving to *Channel Four News* in 1995.

'As editor I'm responsible both editorially and managerially for the news which transmits each weekday night at seven. I am also in charge of bulletins at the weekend, *House to House* (a parliamentary programme transmitted when Parliament is sitting), plus other programmes as commissioned. Each day, with the output editor and team, I decide which topics to cover and how. This starts with a meeting at 9.30. Progress is updated and reviewed throughout the day, specifically at 11.30 and 14.30. After transmission, I review the programme with the team. The rest of the time I struggle with budgets and future coverage.

'The combination of editorial decision-making and general management is extremely stimulating. The job calls for a mind which questions and enjoys being stretched, an ability and interest in structuring items and programmes, a commitment to a large team and a temper that can be kept or lost at will!

'I would advise anyone hoping to work in news to get a good degree, not in media studies but in something tough and rigorous. Don't waste your time at university drinking coffee: *do* something – act, write, play politics. Read the papers and listen to and watch the news – it's amazing how many don't.

'Once you've got into the industry, you need to do more than is expected of you and be more available and willing than anyone else. At least in the first stages of a career, get in early and read everything you can. Don't bluff and never guess – ask if you don't know. Never suggest an idea without thinking of the treatment but suggest lots of ideas. And keep within budget!

'Newsrooms are often macho but actually the problem is being a parent rather than a woman. The hours are long – nearly twelve hours most days – and can be erratic. I would find film-making impossible as it means going away too much. Women in news, like men in news, need wives! Get established and preferably promoted before you have children – it really is a lot harder later.'

Producer

A producer is top dog on a programme and the one in overall charge, managing budgets, organizing resources, deciding on editorial content and leading the team. She is involved at all stages of development: pre-production (general planning and rehearsal, preparing everything for shooting, finding locations, getting a team together, writing and editing scripts, organizing sets), production (recording the programme) and post-production (getting film and sound-tracks into finished shape ready for transmission).

Ultimately responsible if anything goes wrong, a producer oversees everything and has to know at all times what's going on, constantly double-checking that things are going according to plan. When a reporter is recording an interview, the producer may sit in and speak to her over the headphones, telling her what questions to ask. Producers often come up with programme ideas in the first place or develop an idea they're given, then choose their team to work on it. They tend to specialize in a particular type of programme – for example natural history, drama, children's – and to have a relevant background. A producer plays a much more creative role in broadcasting than in the film world, and may function as director too, especially on radio. In fact, teams on radio are so small that the producer may do everything from researching the story to going out and recording it, then mixing it. In local radio, the producer may be presenter, disc jockey, weathercaster and tea-maker. In television, you may be leading a team of forty-odd people.

A producer has to be extremely well organized, good at motivating others and able to blend creative thinking with practical planning and management skills. According to the NUJ, TV producers are generally well paid, with only one in ten earning below £20,000, and 20 per cent on £30,000 or above. On a regional radio station, the range might be more like £16,000–£24,000.

Helen Williams

Age : **37**
Job : **Producer, Granada Television**
Based : **Liverpool**
Salary : **c. £35,000**
Qualifications : **Certificate in Periodical Journalism (LCP)**

'My first job in journalism was as a feature writer on *Eurofruit*, an international magazine for the fruit trade. Yes, really. From there I moved to *Wedding and Home* magazine, went on to edit two titles at the same time, *You and Your Wedding* and *What Diet & Lifestyle*, then became editor of *For Women*. After fourteen years in women's magazines I sat down one weekend, made a list of the aspects of my job I actually enjoyed – and decided I ought to be in TV! So when I saw an ad for a producer for *This Morning*, which is essentially a women's magazine on TV, I applied and got the job.

'A day producer on *This Morning* is responsible for one day a week – that's almost two hours of live, topical TV to fill each week. As producer, working with a team of three researchers, you come up with ideas, book the guests, chase human interest stories, put together the running order, write the script, make VT inserts, edit all clips, liaise with director, props, set design, wardrobe . . . In effect, everything you see on screen for those two hours is only there if you've remembered to do it. It's also the producer's responsibility to make sure all output complies with broadcasting standards and to check out legal implications.

'After eighteen months of this fairly relentless schedule, I'm now producing "strands", series of ten episodes on a particular subject which go out weekly during *This Morning*. This involves travelling round the country with a director, researcher and film crew, setting up locations, interviews, organizing edit schedules and trying to keep a rein on the budget.

'As producer, you have to have enthusiasm and be able to communicate it. You need the ability to juggle, to make instant decisions and to "see" straight away if an item will work.

'I enjoy the adrenalin and the immediacy of live TV. It's the ultimate deadline. There's a great team spirit, akin to working in a war zone sometimes, and the job is very creative and fairly autonomous. On the downside, it's extremely long hours – forget a forty-hour week and think sixty and upwards. And there's lots of paperwork: every actor in every clip, every musician on every backing track, has to be cleared.'

Elaine Gallagher

Age : **32**
Job : **Producer/director, Reuters Television**
Based : **London**
Salary : **£750 a week (freelance)**
Qualifications : **BA (Hons.) Economics**

'I started out on the features desk of *Cosmopolitan* (having previously written for the student section and done work experience there). From there I went to LWT as a researcher on entertainment programmes, then to Mentorn Films as associate producer, eventually becoming the producer responsible for all their arts and entertainment output. I came to Reuters in April 1995.

'It's a two-tier job. I produce *The Entertainment Show*, a weekly magazine programme for Sky News, covering stories from here and America – film premières, celebrity parties, music stories . . . I work out the running order, arrange and direct shoots, edit items, make sure we don't miss out on anything, write scripts, and basically put the whole show together at the end. I also work on an entertainment feed that goes to Reuters' clients around the world.

'The hours are long: never much less than nine thirty to eight or nine at night. When there are premières and parties it's through to midnight, and if you have to feed that material to clients it can be anything up to an eighteen-hour day. It's difficult to have an organized social life and you often have to let people down. I'd love to do something like learn Italian but there's no chance of being able to go to a regular evening class.

'Working in a specific field, you get to know a lot of the other people doing a similar job and, though it's competitive because you're all after the same things, there's quite a good camaraderie. Also, you deal with the same PR people the whole time, so you get to know them fairly well too. Contacts are a very important part of the work – if Clint Eastwood is only doing a set number of interviews you need to be sure you get one of them.

'There isn't a standard career structure or way in – any two people you talk to will probably have a different background. So if you really want to get in and you're persistent, you'll probably do it. I think the basic disciplines are the same throughout all branches of the media: being able to see a story, put it together and make it work. The techniques may vary from print to broadcast but the end aim is the same: you want a lively story that is interesting and well structured and moves along well.'

Sub-editor

In news rooms, subs write copy and rewrite stories from reporters when necessary, as on newspapers. The BBC Monitoring Service also employs sub-editors with language skills to select foreign broadcasts of interest, translate if necessary, sub and write copy.

Continuity Announcer

An announcer supplies the links between programmes, and trails programmes in coming weeks. Announcers also keep viewers informed when programmes are running late, or deliver emergency news bulletins. In addition, an announcer may have other duties such as providing voice-overs and commentaries for other programmes or reading regular news bulletins. Much of the work takes place behind the scenes. They often operate technical equipment and write their own scripts (though some have them prepared by scriptwriters). They also have to be aware of and prepared for any hiccups that may throw out normal transmission so they need to be able to think on their feet. On fortunately rare occasions, technical glitches might interrupt service, in which case an ability to ad lib convincingly is invaluable.

They are the public voice – and sometimes, especially in the ITV regions, the face – of the station. The image they present is therefore all-important, and will vary from region to region, depending on the station's own image. Certain qualities are essential, though: a clear, pleasant voice, smart and attractive appearance, likeable personality and air of authority. The way they introduce a programme can influence how many viewers stay tuned to watch it so it's a responsible role.

Recruitment ads for television announcers attract floods of applicants – the job has such a glamorous image, offers a degree of fame and recognition and looks so easy to do, but most announcers have trained in speech and drama or journalism, or had experience in the entertainment industry or in teaching. There are very few vacancies for inexperienced applicants.

Scriptwriter

A scriptwriter works behind the scenes, writing up news stories for transmission and liaising with reporters and technical staff on accompanying graphics and captions, etc. A promotion scriptwriter works on the trailers for forthcoming programmes and on scripts for continuity announcers, who provide links between programmes. The term is also used to describe people who write the scripts for dramas and soap operas (see p. 72).

Runner

Runners are general dogsbodies, who do anything and everything asked of them – running errands, making tea, answering the phones, taking messages, etc. It's usually long and tiring work for which you are paid a pittance – but it's a way in and a chance to see what goes on and to meet people. Even at this level, jobs are hard to come by: many use this as a first step.

Subtitler

Subtitling, often done by sub-editors, involves editing the speech content of a television programme into concise, easily read captions while retaining the sense and flavour of the production. You need to work quickly and accurately. Entry is at graduate level and usually after editing experience elsewhere.

Starting salaries would generally be around £19,000.

Researcher

A researcher comes up with ideas for items on a programme, researches the subjects thoroughly, then 'sells' them to the rest of the team. If they are working on a chat show, for example, they would think of possible interviewees, track them down, research each guest's personal history and perhaps carry out initial interviews, and prepare questions and briefings for the interviewer. On a quiz or game show they could be writing and checking questions, arranging auditions or screening contestants. The work may include editing and checking facts for accuracy or writing linking copy and short scripts. They might also find unusual pictures or old film footage, trawl through archives for facts and information, come up with suggestions for shooting locations and generally act in an investigative capacity.

Researchers in specialist areas, such as natural history or science programmes, are expected to have an in-depth knowledge of their field and all researchers need to know how to make themselves well informed for the short-term – where to find information, contacts, etc. Much of the time may be spent on the phone, trying to track down people and information. In radio, researchers may also act as producers (but without the extra money!).

This is an extremely popular route into journalism and competition is fierce, particularly for advertised vacancies. Once you're in, competition is still intense – research is full of bright young things eager to prove themselves and move on to become producers. Most researchers are graduates, many with experience in other areas of the media, but the most important qualifications are enthusiasm, an outgoing and curious nature, initiative and motivation. You also need to be well organized and accurate, and to read newspapers and magazines constantly on the look-out for ideas. The jobs are often given on short-term contracts, which may be for as little as six weeks or three months. Average salaries for TV or radio researchers are around £14,000 to £20,000.

Julia Carrington

Age : **27**
Job : **TV researcher, Anglia Television**
Based : **Norwich**
Salary range : **£15–20,000**
Qualifications : **BA (Hons.) Modern Languages; Postgraduate Diploma in Radio and Television Journalism**

'I started as a voluntary hockey reporter working in BBC local radio. I stood around the pitch compiling live reports to broadcast on a portable phone. I knew nothing about hockey – always stood near a hockey buff – and always got freezing cold hands! But it was a start and has proved to be worth it.

'I think showing initiative definitely leads to getting a job. I got my current job by writing to the editor of *The Time The Place*, asking about the future possibility of employment, before any jobs were advertised. It is well worth writing to the editors of different TV programmes or the managing editor of your local BBC radio station, asking for a chance to do work experience or come in for a day to look at what goes on.

'Thursday is my programme day. After the programme goes out at 10.30 a.m., the senior producer, producer and I look through papers and consider ideas. I might do some preliminary research to see whether a subject is going to be difficult to work on or not. I look at cuttings, papers and magazines, and talk to friends and other journalists to see whether something good is happening. Once the editor has decided on a programme I get down to making calls.

'You have to be persistent, polite but firm, and be good at thinking around a subject to see how it would make a good discussion programme. For example, an article on women obsessed with Marti Pellow led to a discussion on putting up with your partner.

'The downside of the job is all the administration – faxing information to people, booking train tickets, calculating petrol costs and ringing up guests to check they have the details they need and are not going to back out of the programme. The best bit is making a successful programme. I enjoy the buzz of getting hold of someone no one else has been able to and I like interviewing people on the phone and persuading them they are good enough to come on the television. Researching is a bit like swinging on branches through the jungle! You have to weave your way around to get to what you want.'

Deborah Dudgeon

Age : **26**
Job : **Researcher, magazine programmes, BBC Radio**
Based : **London**
Salary : **c. £19,000**
Qualifications : **BA (Hons.) Psychology; Postgraduate Diploma in Journalism**

'I got really involved in the paper at university (initially because I fancied someone who worked on it) then did a postgraduate journalism course. After that I worked briefly at *Mountain Biking UK*, before going to *Radio Times* as a features researcher. I left after eighteen months to work freelance as a reporter, writer, researcher and sub, then joined the BBC in 1994.

'As a researcher I move around: I've been on three different programmes in nine months – *Breakaway*, *Going Places* and now *You and Yours* – and I could easily be sent to another one next month. On some programmes researchers just do the research, then hand it over to a producer. On others they act as producers, which is what I'm doing at the moment – so I get to do recording and editing too, which is really good fun. Most of the time you're office-bound but I love it when you can go out and about and interview people.

'On *You and Yours* there's a meeting at 8.30, by which time we're meant to have read the papers. We discuss the features that are going to be on and suggest changes and improvements, so if you've got something on that day's programme you're then really busy up to twelve o'clock. If you've arranged for a guest to come in, you go down to the studio and help the presenter because you probably interviewed the person on the phone initially so you know what they're going to say. Otherwise, most of the day is spent on the phone, trying to structure a story, finding out who the right people to talk to are, then arranging to interview them.

'Working on daily programmes is stressful. You're really busy up till the programme goes out, then you start frantically preparing for the next one, knowing you've got less than twenty-four hours to try and get people to come on live. It's very satisfying if you find a great story and get the people you want to talk about it, or if you do a good recording or a good mix in the studio. But it's rather like a factory, churning it out – once you've done one story, it's straight on to the next.'

PA (Production Assistant)

A PA provides administrative and secretarial support to the producer and director, liaising between them and the rest of the team. She is responsible for booking studios, rehearsal rooms, equipment, hotels and cars; arranging contracts; keeping records; typing up scripts and schedules and distributing them; making sure crew and cast know where to be and when; and generally acting as a co-ordinator. Some of these tasks may be shared with a production secretary, if the programme is large enough. Along with the producer, the PA is a central figure on any programme and a point of contact for all involved. Unlike other members of the team who may be involved in only pre-production or production, the PA usually stays from start to finish.

One of the PA's most important roles on a live programme is timing all the items with a stop-watch and making sure producer and presenters know how much time is left and whether anything will have to be cut. On live TV programmes, she sits in the gallery with the director, relaying her instructions to the team on the floor and cueing in sound and video packages. On drama productions, where scenes are shot out of sequence, the PA usually also acts as the continuity person, ensuring consistency from one scene to another. If the programme does fact sheets the PA may write those. She may also do research, especially if there is no researcher on the programme. Depending on the programme, the job can be largely studio-based or may call for frequent time away on location.

As well as possessing great organizational and secretarial skills, a PA must be able to work to deadline, be unflappable under stress, and be good at thinking on her feet and finding a way round problems. She must be meticulous, pay attention to detail and possess great communication skills and the ability to get on with lots of people, however big or frail their egos. A head for figures is also important when it comes to timing programmes and keeping an eye on the running time.

Salaries for PAs would usually be several thousand pounds less than those paid to researchers.

Presenter

Presenters' backgrounds and characteristics are as wide and varied as the programmes they present. Some are established 'personalities' called in to front a programme; others are hired because they've acquired expertise in a relevant area. A wild and wacky game show, for example, might be presented by someone with an acting or other entertainment background; news and current-affairs presenters tend to have started as reporters or to have a background in print or radio journalism; sports commentators are often familiar as former sportsmen and women.

Presenting jobs are rarely advertised, though there are exceptions. When public auditions *are* held, they attract massive numbers of eager applicants.

Personality and good communication skills are important for a presenter, as well as bags of confidence and calmness under pressure. They need to be able to draw out extra interesting stories from guests and interviewees, especially on radio where they have to make a story come alive with words only. For television presenting, an attractive personal appearance and good dress sense are important, unless you're such a well-known expert in your field that you've risen above all that.

Salaries vary widely – a novice broadcaster on a small ILR or community station may get as little as £8 per hour, but for the big names in the business, the sky's the limit, and earnings can be boosted by doing personal appearances, speeches, etc.

Shahnaz Pakravan

Age : **38**
Job : **Presenter/reporter, BBC Television**
Based : **London**
Salary range : **£50–75,000**
Qualifications : **BA Theatre Arts and Psychology**

'I trained as a reporter/news presenter with Dubai TV but my break in British television came in 1987 when I joined BBC TV in Norwich as presenter on a regional current affairs programme. In 1988 I moved to BBC Pebble Mill to present a weekly Asian magazine programme, *Network East*. I left in 1989 so I wouldn't pigeonhole myself into the "Asian" mould; to prove I could make it in mainstream TV without a colour or racial tag. It was a huge gamble but proved to be the right decision. From 1991 I worked as a newscaster with Channel 4, also presenting a health programme, *The Pulse*. In 1994 I returned to the BBC as a reporter on *Tomorrow's World*; now I co-present the show as well as continuing to make weekly films.

'The versatility of my job is great. I travel extensively, meeting interesting people and covering exciting new developments in science and technology. The work involves researching stories, writing scripts, making contact with contributors, then going on location to film. UK stories can take up to three filming days; foreign trips obviously take longer. One of the best (and toughest) moments was filming in Siberia, in the world's coldest city, Yakutsk, where temperatures dropped to −46. Doing pieces to camera when your mouth is nearly freezing is a feat unto itself!

'As I also present in the studio, Thursdays are always taken up putting the programme together, starting at 9 a.m. with script meetings. That's followed by any commentary recordings for specific films, then it's into make-up and costume and on to the set for two hours to record the links for the show.

'If you want to work in television, you have to have heaps of patience and the right amount of push – then get yourself heard and seen by those who matter. It's tough and it's competitive, so don't give up if it doesn't magically happen straight away. Once in, it's important to have staying power because there will be rejections and disappointments. Keep your contacts with people fresh because you never know who you will need at what stage of your career. And always be good to everybody on the way up because you might need them on the way down!'

Scriptwriter/Editor

In many cases (on documentaries and current affairs programmes, for example) producers and researchers write their own scripts. On other programmes such as drama and soap operas, this is done by scriptwriters, who may either come up with an original idea themselves or be commissioned to write or adapt an existing work. Scriptwriters are generally freelance and often successful authors in their own right. They work with the producer and director to translate text and ideas into something that will work visually.

Script editors work on drama productions, from classic serials such as *Pride and Prejudice* to soap operas such as *Coronation Street*. On the soaps, where different writers contribute scripts for different episodes, the script editor will work with them to ensure there's an overall uniformity and harmony. Other script editors appraise unsolicited scripts sent in by eager would-be screenplay writers or read novels and comment on how well they could transfer to screen or radio. Once a script is in production, a script editor may have to go on location with the rest of the crew, so that she's on hand during filming to accommodate any late changes that may need to be made to the script if problems occur. Many script editors have had experience in other areas of journalism first.

Secretaries

Competition for secretarial jobs is intense and many applicants are graduates who see this as a way in to broadcasting. It is *not* a guaranteed stepping stone to greater things but is definitely not to be knocked and is a valuable way to get an overall understanding of how things work. Many extremely successful women in television started their careers as secretaries – though there are many others who would complain that they got stuck in the secretarial rut and couldn't get on. Certainly, no one will be impressed by a secretary who's so ambitious to get on that she neglects her proper work, so you have to be prepared to handle all the normal secretarial duties efficiently and well, even if it's not your long-term career goal. You'll be running an office, handling correspondence and calls, typing, arranging meetings, etc. If you're working on a programme, you may undertake some of the duties of the production assistant (see p. 69), but secretarial openings on programmes are hard to come by and you are more likely to start off in an administrative or programme support area. Within the BBC, some secretaries work as relief staff, moving wherever they are needed at a particular time, which gives a chance to try out different departments.

Lis Howell

Age : **44**
Job : **Director of Programmes, UK Living**
Based : **London**
Salary : **£70–80,000**
Qualifications : **BA (Hons.) English**

'After university, I went to America as part of an expedition travel-ling down the coast. We got interviewed by lots of local radio and TV stations and I thought, "This is great – that's what I want to do." So when I came back I enrolled in a media studies course and while I was there got a Saturday morning tea-girl job on the local radio station, BBC Radio Leeds. After six months they gave me a one-year contract as a reporter and eventually I became co-presenter, then producer.

'From there I went to Border TV, then Granada, then Tyne Tees. After time out when my daughter was born, I returned to work as Head of News at Border and became Deputy Programme Controller in 1988. The following year I joined Sky News as Managing Editor, left to become Director of Programmes for the launch of GMTV, then moved to *Good Morning with Anne and Nick*. In 1993 I was asked to develop the concept that became UK Living.

'I was the very first person employed on the channel, so I've seen it growing and that's wonderful. I'm responsible for all of its content except the ad breaks. It's a huge job and was very hard at first, just putting a schedule together and praying it would work, but once you get going it's great because you have certain building blocks – two hours every day for our live programme, a film every night, some quizzes. A lot of the time now I just tweak the sched-ule. I look at other programmes to buy, devise big events and campaigns, come up with ideas. It's very strategic, always thinking six months ahead.

'Till the day I die, quarter past to half past ten in the morning will be different for me than for other people because that's when ratings come in, every single morning. With magazines you have to wait months for the circulation figures, but here you get a feel for things really fast. At first I used to dread it but now I find it exciting. You can see things starting to work, programmes slowly build. And that's really satisfying. It's great having the power to make changes and seeing the results.'

Getting into Radio and Television

In this highly competitive industry, good qualifications aren't enough – in fact, they're pretty much taken for granted and most entrants are graduates. A Skillset survey of freelances in broadcasting found that 82 per cent had a degree or diploma.

Just as Fleet Street journalists tend to start in the regional press, so most broadcast journalists begin their career on a local radio station. Teams on radio programmes are much smaller than in TV, so you'll get experience of many different tasks. TV staff are recruited almost entirely from people already qualified and experienced in radio or newspapers.

The most important thing for beginners is to be able to demonstrate commitment to and interest in broadcasting. There are a number of ways in which you can do this:

• Get as much practical experience as you can by working for a student station, volunteering on hospital or community radio, etc. A recent issue of the CRA's *Airflash* claimed that 'at least a fifth of people currently employed in mainstream radio began their careers by working as unpaid volunteers, mostly in student, hospital or community radio.'

• Watch TV or listen to the radio and know what you're talking about. If you want to be a researcher, study the programme you're interested in then write to the producer with ideas for future programmes, giving a brief synopsis of how you would tackle the subject and who you'd talk to.

• Grab every opportunity to see how things work behind the

scenes. Try to go along to studio recordings; tickets are often advertised in local papers and listings magazines, or, for BBC programmes, write, enclosing a stamped addressed envelope, to Radio Ticket Unit, BBC, London WIA 4WW, or Television Ticket Unit, BBC, London WI2 7SB. See if you can get any work as an extra.

• Contact TV and radio stations to see if they'd give you a behind-the-scenes tour. Visit places like the Granada Studios Tour (in Manchester), the Museum of the Moving Image (London) and the National Museum of Photography, Film and Television (Bradford).

• Volunteer to help out on special appeals, such as Comic Relief and Children in Need, when spare hands are often needed to answer phones or stuff envelopes for mailing factsheets. You won't get paid but it's a perfect chance to see some of what goes on, have direct contact with both listeners and presenters, and maybe meet some useful people.

• If you're a student, make the most of the opportunity to learn to make and edit films with the film society or get involved in producing for the amateur dramatics society.

• Ask if you can supply freelance reports to the local radio station.

• Look out for TV programmes such as *Video Diaries* that supply members of the public with camcorders to make short films about their lives – if you can convince them you'd make a good story, this is a perfect way to get experience and catch people's eye.

• Be aware of technological and other changes and the kind of impact they will have on the industry.

Training Schemes

The BBC runs three top-notch journalism training schemes: (1) regional news trainee scheme (television); (2) local radio trainee journalist scheme; (3) news trainee scheme (bi-media). All three are hotly competed for, attracting thousands of applicants every year for just twelve places on each. Graduates are preferred, additional formal training is an advantage and evidence of relevant work experience is a must.

The BBC also has trainee schemes for television production, World Service production, radio production and news. For details of trainee schemes, write to the Appointments Officer at Broadcasting House (see Chapter 12).

Some of the ITV companies have occasional structured trainee journalist schemes for beginners, but it depends on each company's staffing situation. Unsurprisingly, competition for places on these schemes, which are usually advertised in the national press, is fierce.

ITN admits a small number of graduates on its graduate editorial trainee scheme each year and looks for applicants with a good knowledge of current affairs, a passion for journalism and relevant work experience, which can be in print, radio or TV. They recruit annually in February, and advertise at universities and in the *Guardian*. For details of the scheme, contact the Training Department, ITN Ltd, 200 Grays Inn Road, London WC1X 8XZ.

Chapter 4 / **Book Publishing**

Book publishing in Britain is a £3 billion a year industry, which, despite a deep recession in the trade, is still producing more books than ever before, mostly paperbacks. In 1994 alone, over 89,000 new titles were issued.

The largest sector is 'trade' publishing, the industry term for general consumer titles, both fiction and non-fiction, which accounts for 60 per cent of UK sales. But there is also a big market for academic and educational books: think of how many subjects are studied in schools and universities, all supported by recommended textbooks, and you'll realize how big a market it is. Then there are professional fields such as law and medicine, all with their own specialist books. Children's books, too, are thriving. Another major growth area is in audio books, whose sales are said to be trebling every year.

The development of electronic publishing and entertainment is having a huge impact on the industry. Publishers are realizing the potential offered by multimedia, particularly in the reference sector. CD-ROM allows vast memory reserves of text, pictures, animations, video and sound to be carried on a single disk, with obvious huge advantages over traditional reference books in terms of storage space, portability and search facilities. Dorling Kindersley has been leading the way and other publishers are eagerly investigating the possibilities. The BBC, for example, has been developing CD-ROMs in wildlife, language learning, children's entertainment and other genres.

One of the biggest changes to hit the publishing industry in recent years was the abolition in September 1995 of the Net Book Agreement, the publishers' cartel that, for almost a hundred years, fixed the selling price of books at an agreed minimum amount. At the time of going to press, it remains to be seen quite how great will be the consequences. Supporters of the NBA warned that it could mean hundreds of smaller, independent bookshops being forced out of business, unable to compete with the discounting power of the giant chains, as happened in France where 20 per cent of shops closed down. Critics of the Agreement, however, viewed it as a victory for the reading public and were expecting book sales to boom as prices dropped, citing the example of Australia, where abandonment of fixed prices led to no drastic change.

There is also the ever-recurring threat of VAT being imposed on books, which would undoubtedly lead to a further fall in book sales. In addition, there has been much concern (and publicity) about the huge advances paid out to one or two big-name authors – such as Martin Amis and Jeffrey Archer – and fears that this would leave no margin for publishers to invest in first-time novelists.

Publishers look to make the big money not from sales alone but from tie-in serializations, and film and foreign rights. They also try to sell titles to book clubs, who then offer them to their members at a discounted price; they may do their own print run or take stock from the publisher but either way the publisher is happy at a guaranteed number of sales.

Publishers aim to 'build lists', that is, to develop a range of titles in a certain field. Backlists – books already published and still in print – should ideally be titles that continue to earn money and are regularly reprinted, although they can also include copies of titles that didn't sell and are left over. Every publisher hopes to have good, popular names on their backlist to carry on providing a steady income – and they'd kill for a Delia Smith or John le Carré, whose books just carry on selling and selling. At the same time, they should be looking to develop new, up-and-coming authors, who they hope will turn into profitable backlist material eventually.

The numbers of editorial staff working on a book will vary. A novel may have just a commissioning editor and desk editor involved. A big reference book, on the other hand, would require the services of a large team, including researchers, writers, editors, subs and picture researchers, and consequently, is a much larger investment on the part of the publisher. Annual publications have to be produced quickly and under pressure, yet no less accurately, and must be as up to date as possible. In some areas new technology can help speed up the process.

The UK publishing industry employs around 22,000 people, although in recent years, like many industries, it has been subject to increased rationalization, and consequent cutbacks in jobs. There have been a confusing number of takeovers and mergers since the 1980s and it's no easy task to keep track of who owns what. Many of the smaller houses (as publishing firms are generally known) have been swallowed up by larger international companies that own several imprints and lists. The country's three largest publishers, HarperCollins, Random House and Penguin Books, between them sell more than half the books in Britain. Yet there are still mavericks who, now and then, spot a gap in the market for a certain type of book and break away to found their own specialist houses, which, in turn, may sell out to larger houses eager to add a particular list to their portfolios. According to the 1996 edition of *The Writers' Handbook*, in the UK there are around 6,000 small presses and publishers.

As in other areas of media, there has also been a drive towards using more freelances, most of them former in-house staff, in a bid to cut overheads. Even for those on staff, book publishing is notoriously badly paid, especially in the smaller, more radical companies – it's not an area you go into to make your fortune. However, there can be attractive perks such as free and discounted books, and launch parties. Like the rest of the media, it is largely concentrated in and around London.

There are strong links between publishers and other media because they rely to a great extent on free publicity for their books via reviews in newspapers, magazines, TV and radio programmes. The publicity department will send authors on rounds of interviews to tie in with new releases, arrange book readings and signings in book stores, giveaways and competitions in magazines, etc.

The main functions within publishing are editorial, production and design (the process of manufacturing and printing the book), marketing (sales and publicity), and distribution, but in this book we are looking only at those journalism-related jobs that make up the editorial side. This is generally the area in which most people are interested, although it has fewer openings than the other areas. As ever, job titles are flexible and vary from company to company. The larger the house, the greater the chance of specializing. In a smaller one, the roles of commissioning editor, copy editor and proofreader can all be filled by one person.

The Job Descriptions

Editorial Director

At the top of the editorial tree comes the editorial or publishing director, with a seat on the board. Having reached this stage, she will usually be less involved in hands-on editing of individual books and more concerned with overseeing the whole publishing process, though she may also continue to commission books. An editorial director will attend meetings with editorial, design and publicity staff to discuss plans and progress. She approves copy for covers, catalogue, press releases and advance information and, along with other members of the board, is involved in strategic thinking about ways to increase the company's turnover.

In a major publishing house, an editorial director's salary would probably be around the £40,000 mark.

Kathy Gale

Age : **35**
Job : **Joint Managing Director and Publishing Director, The Women's Press**
Based : **London**
Salary : **'a lot lower than it would be in a mainstream publishing house or for a comparative position in most other businesses'**
Qualifications : **BA (Hons.) English Literature**

'After university I had no idea what I wanted to do so I joined a college bookshop on a temporary basis, then, when that ran out, joined the W. H. Smith nearest my flat on a management training scheme. I worked in two of the largest branches of WHS for just under a year, gaining an excellent front-line sense of how books got sold from the largest and most influential book chain.

'I began to see that publishing would be an interesting way to go, so I then moved to J. Whitaker & Sons as an assistant bibliographer. For a year I transferred information about books from one form to another and proofread long bibliographical printouts. It was a hugely boring job but good proofreading training. I then worked as a copy editor at Pan Books and as managing editor at Pluto Press before taking my first commissioning job with Hodder & Stoughton. Then I was headhunted twice – the only way to get a decent salary in book publishing – and, the third time, went to Pan Macmillan as senior commissioning editor, where I later became editorial director. In June 1991 I was approached by The Women's Press for my current job – a post which reflected my politics and made good use of my experience. Home!

'On a typical day I am likely to be: in a series of meetings; at my desk, trying desperately to catch up on correspondence and telephone calls to authors, agents and other publishers; looking over catalogue, cover, advance information, rights guide, press release, publicity campaigns and other copy; choosing an illustrator or assessing an illustrator's roughs for a cover; editing books; working with my colleague Mary Hemming on sales or expenditure figures and thinking of future strategies for the company. I am also training other women at The Press to commission and edit.

'There are far too few hours in the day and days in the week to do everything we have to do. But The Women's Press is continuing to thrive, which is very important to me, and it is an immense privilege to work in a job that you believe to be important. That's my greatest satisfaction.'

Commissioning Editor

This is a key editorial job in book publishing and the one to which most entrants aspire. Commissioning editors decide whether or not a book will be published, choosing which to reject and which to accept of the hundreds of manuscripts and proposals sent to them. Sometimes, in the case of a recognized author, they may buy a book before it has even been written, just on the basis of an outline. The vast majority of the unsolicited manuscripts they are sent – from individuals and from literary agents acting on behalf of clients – end up on the reject pile. Fewer than 2 per cent are likely to go any further.

A commissioning editor also initiates books, so needs to identify opportunities and market trends, keeping an eye open for what's selling, which way the market is going, where there are gaps crying out to be filled. If she has an idea for a project, she will research it to find out how it is likely to sell. If it looks like a goer, she must then find and commission an author to do it, agreeing with them what the scope and contents of the book will be and negotiating the payment and delivery date for the manuscript. In some cases, she may also be liaising with authors' agents. She will oversee the issuing of contracts with the contracts and rights department.

Throughout the publishing process, the commissioning editor continues to keep in close contact with the author, checking progress, chivvying and chasing if necessary, giving feedback on the manuscript so far, maybe suggesting changes, encouraging when the author is flagging, sending them rough designs and copy (blurb) for the cover, and so on, for their comments and approval. The relationship between an author and commissioning editor is an important one – when an editor transfers to another publishing house, authors often want to follow them.

When the manuscript has been received, the commissioning editor reads it to see that it is the book she asked for, then continues to oversee it throughout the editing and production process. That will include briefing the art department as to cover design and any illustrations that have to be commissioned. She may write the blurbs for the book jacket and catalogue, or approve that written by the publicity department. In the case of a senior author, the commissioning editor may also edit the book herself; otherwise, she would hand it over to a copy editor or desk editor to deal with under her supervision.

Commissioning editors need to read widely and have a real feel for what the reading public wants. They have to be creative and full of ideas. If working for an academic or professional publisher you need specialist knowledge of the area. You must be tactful, too, to be able to deal with authors who may be upset at the changes you suggest.

It can be satisfying to help an author produce a bestseller or to build a quality backlist. However, as well as the creative aspects, the job also involves setting budgets and trying to prioritize and juggle tasks when you have several projects on the go at once. It can also be stressful trying to keep to deadlines, especially as authors are notorious – even worse than journalists – when it comes to delivering copy on time.

The average salary for a commissioning editor is around £20–£30,000.

Sally Abbey

Age : **29**
Job : **Commissioning editor, Hamish Hamilton/Penguin Books**
Based : **London**
Salary range : **£20–25,000**
Qualifications : **BA English Literature**

'When I left university I realized all my so-called "qualifications" were getting me absolutely nowhere without keyboard skills or work experience. What did I do? I took a word-processing course, embroidered the truth on my CV, really worked for the interview and got a job.

'I started out as an administrator for a design company, then worked as a publicity executive for various retail outlets before realizing, two years after university, that I needed to make a career decision. Books and reading were what I wanted to do, so I took a step down in seniority and salary to join Penguin Books as an editorial secretary in 1989. I found the job via a specialist recruitment agency. Once you're in, getting ahead is largely a matter of being in the right place at the right time. After eighteen months I became an assistant editor at Hamish Hamilton and was promoted to my current position in 1995.

'I commission new titles for the Hamish Hamilton (hardback) list and also buy books for Penguin. Much of my time is spent talking to authors on the phone – encouraging them, hassling them about deadlines and making sure I am representing their best interests in-house. I brief the design department about the cover design, the contracts department about the specific terms of the agreement and the sales force so they know exactly how to pitch the books when they sell the new titles into the shops.

'You need to have a good eye for genuinely original writing. The best thing about this job is being sent a manuscript or proposal which is really exceptional. The sense of being on the verge of discovering the new Donna Tartt or Iain Banks is a great thrill.

'The downsides of the job are the long hours, endless reading, and being nice to difficult authors. It's also hard trying to sell hardback fiction in the current economic climate. And it's a fairly sexist industry – whilst it's female-dominated at a certain level, few make it to the top.'

Christine Winters

Age : **29**
Job : **Editorial lead, Dorling Kindersley**
Based : **London**
Salary : **confidential**
Qualifications : **BA (Hons.) Philosophy and Social and Political Sciences**

'While other people went travelling, I spent my summers at university doing the rounds of magazines, newspapers and book publishers, slogging away working for no money. I probably got my first job (as an editorial assistant with a military history publisher) because I'd already been in an office and knew various publishing terms and things you only find out from working in-house. After that I became a desk editor at Routledge, an academic publisher, and stayed there for three years, moving up to senior desk editor, before going to HarperCollins as an editor in the further education department. From there I moved to Guinness Publishing and produced encyclopaedias.

'By then I became aware that reference book publishing was beginning to look a bit out of date compared to what CD-ROMs are capable of, so I moved into multimedia as one of a team of editors on Microsoft's Encarta. Then I was offered this job at Dorling Kindersley, working on a major CD-ROM project, the *Eyewitness Encyclopedia of Space and The Universe*.

'I have a team of five editors and an editorial assistant and work closely with a design lead, who has about the same number of designers. We also co-ordinate animators, video and sound engineers, software people and production people, as well as outside consultants employed for their expertise in a particular subject.

'I commission text from contributors, just as you would with a book or magazine, and oversee it as it comes through, rewriting any bits that need it. The design lead and I also commission the animations, working out which bits to illustrate and how to do it. Captions, annotations and animation and narration scripts are generally written in-house by the editors. If a subject is very specialized, a consultant might suggest what to include and the editor writes around that then gets the consultant to check it.

'The skills in multimedia aren't that different from those used on books – you just have to add to them. I'd never worked with narration scripts or edited video before, for example. And all the screen text is narrated as well as put on screen so when writing or editing copy you need to think about how it will sound, not just how it reads. I often find myself mumbling while I'm writing, which I didn't do before!'

Copy Editor/Desk Editor

Once a manuscript has been accepted, the commissioning editor will pass it on to a desk editor to prepare it for publication. The desk editor may also work on titles bought from foreign publishers, polishing up a translation or anglicizing American English. As the title desk editor suggests, this is very much an office-bound job.

The job is essentially the same as that of a sub-editor on a newspaper or magazine. A desk editor reads a typescript for clarity and accuracy, weeding out spelling and grammatical errors, checking that there are no repetitions, contradictions or missing chunks of text. She makes sure that the pictures and words tally and that the texts conform to house style. She liaises with the author on any changes that need to be made or querying anything that seems suspect. She may be responsible for overseeing indexing and proofreading, and liaising with design teams, commissioning editors and typesetters.

Precision and attention to detail are vital and, of course, an excellent command of English grammar, spelling and punctuation. And you have to have respect for other people's work and be able to deal sensitively with an author's text, not changing it just because it's not to your personal taste. You also need to have a good general knowledge so that you can tell if something doesn't look right and know how to check it. Concentration, dedication and a high boredom threshold are vital, as you may have to work for long spells on a single manuscript.

Editing is increasingly done on screen or may be done on hard copy for the changes to be later taken in on disk by someone else (maybe the typesetter or author). Changes on hard copy must be made clearly so there's no confusion, so legible handwriting is important. You also need to know the typesetting correction symbols used when marking up text (see Chapter 8).

When editing has been done and corrections taken in, proofs are then sent out to the author and editor for reading. The simpler the book, the quicker the editing process – a novel, for example, would be much simpler to edit than a complicated text or reference book with lots of tables, photos and illustrations, which might have to go through several proof stages.

A copy editor would probably earn around £15–20,000.

Mary-Rose Doherty

Age : **38**
Job : **Assistant editor, HarperCollins Publishers**
Based : **London**
Salary : ***c.* £16–17,000**
Qualifications : **courses in business studies, copy editing and book publishing**

'From 1976 to 1985 I was features secretary at the *Sunday Mirror*, working for the showbusiness editor, television reviewer, film and theatre critic, political editor, chief crime reporter and gossip columnist – a hectic and very enjoyable job. I then moved to News International to be promotions assistant for the *Sun* and the *News of the World*, which involved everything from administering weekly competitions in the two newspapers to helping organize and attend a wide variety of media events.

'I then worked in temporary secretarial positions for various media companies before joining HarperCollins in 1987. I worked here as a secretary to the paperback publishing director and as an editorial assistant for two editorial directors before commencing my present role three years ago.

'I work in the fiction department of the Trade Division reporting to, and providing support to, an editorial director who publishes a wide range of highly commercial novels and some literary fiction. A typical day can vary from one spent editing continuously on-screen to a highly diverse one consisting of any of the following tasks: putting books into production; collating proofs; briefing the art department on the cover approach for jackets; writing cover copy or other promotional material for forthcoming titles; proofreading jackets; clearing permissions for material reproduced in novels; and creating acquisition forms for potential new novels (that is, getting together a stunning résumé of why we should buy the next sure-fire bestseller and circulating it to the people who matter).

'The job is desk-bound, and it can get monotonous if one is looking at proofs all day. The link with authors is rather tenuous and unless you're at a more senior level you don't get the opportunity to entertain authors or nurture their writing careers. But on the plus side, we get half-price books in-house and a reduction on other publishers' books. There are publication parties and readings where we get to meet authors, and occasional film and television screenings when we do a book tie-in for an adaptation. The best bits are having the opportunity to work on novels by famous authors and seeing finished copies of books that you've worked on, especially on display in bookshops and being read by members of the public.'

Proofreader

Most proofreaders are freelances with previous in-house publishing experience. As their name suggests, they read proofs with an eagle eye for errors, double-checking for accuracy at all levels, for matching up of captions to pictures, etc. In some instances, the copy editor and proofreader are the same person.

See page 95 for typical freelance payment rates.

Reader

Some publishing houses employ freelance readers to look through unsolicited manuscripts and submit written assessments on them, earmarking any that might be of interest. Most will be unpublishable, but all must be read, just in case there's a major new talent lurking in among them. Readers are generally people with previous publishing experience and an eye for good writing and what's likely to sell.

Getting into Book Publishing

Although some training courses are available (see Chapter 9), there is not the same emphasis on pre-entry training as in other branches of the media, and most entrants to book publishing generally come in straight from college or university and learn the trade on the job. Most are graduates, but don't assume that you have to have a literature-based degree: there are many specialist and academic publishers where training in medicine, architecture or the law, for example, will be more relevant.

Anyone planning to go into publishing should get to know the style of the publisher they're applying to (we give a brief idea of major publishers' specialities in Chapter 13). For example, if you want to work on literary fiction, don't waste your time applying to a company renowned for its travel guides.

As with all areas of the media, and despite the low salaries on offer, publishing is hugely popular as a career choice, so you need to grab any chance of acquiring relevant experience. Working in a bookshop is a start, even if just at weekends or in the holidays. It will give you valuable hands-on experience of how books are marketed, what readers want, what's shifting and what's sticking. You will get a feel for the different publishers and their books. Be warned, though, that bookshops are inundated with applicants and jobs are rarely advertised, as many already have waiting lists. Other good places to try for work experience are libraries or other branches of the media.

Within the industry, first jobs are usually as secretaries or editorial assistants, providing administrative and secretarial support to editors. The skills needed in these jobs (typing, using computers) will stand you in good stead as you progress, as books are increasingly edited on screen. You may also be given some basic editorial tasks to do, such as research or fact-checking.

This is very much a graduate-dominated profession and even at entry level, you will be expected to have a degree. Starting off in a small publisher's is the best way to gain all-round experience of a variety of tasks, but larger houses are more likely to offer training and use more advanced systems.

Take the chance to visit any book fairs and festivals such as Hay-on-Wye or the Edinburgh Book Festival (next to be held in August 1997). Go to book readings. Follow reviews in the press and read as much as you can. Look at book club ads in newspapers and magazines to see which titles are being promoted.

There are a number of industry conferences you can attend, run by organizations such as Women in Publishing and Book House. Or you can enrol on training courses which, as well as teaching you practical skills, will start you off with contacts.

Chapter 5 / **Working as a Freelance**

Freelances do not need any particular educational or journalism qualifications. However, most people are unwilling to take a chance on anyone without a proven track record, and to make a real go of freelance work, you need a solid network of contacts who will keep a steady stream of work coming your way. It is therefore most usual for people to be professional and experienced journalists before they decide to go freelance.

There are opportunities for freelances in all sorts of areas but whatever your field, there are certain points to bear in mind if you want to be successful.

• Getting paid is almost always a hassle and if you can't cope with invoicing and chasing payments, you're not going to hack it as a freelance. Invoice as soon as possible after the work is completed, giving the date, invoice number, brief description of the job or title of the article; the name of the person who booked or commissioned you; the agreed fee plus expenses if relevant; to whom cheques should be made payable and your name and address. Don't feel guilty or embarrassed about chasing if payments are slow – this is your livelihood. Most unions (for example, NUJ, BECTU (see Chapter 10)) offer their members a debt-chasing or collecting service, which is especially useful for freelances.

• Agree on deadline and payment *before* you do any work, and get it in writing. If you're working in the company's offices, make sure you're paid regularly – either weekly or on the monthly payroll. Don't, for example, agree to do six weeks' work for a lump sum at the end.

• Keep an eye on the trade press and check out job ads: if a company is recruiting, it may be short-staffed and keen to use freelances.

• Be reliable and do every job to the best of your ability. Remember that this is a relatively small business and people talk to each other. A good reputation gets around, but so does a bad one.

• Get equipped! An answering machine is vital if you don't want to lose work. For writers, a computer is essential and a fax machine is increasingly expected. You can rent a fax machine, just as you do your phone; alternatively, a local print or office supplies shop might accept incoming faxes for you for a fee. The really switched-on will have a modem, so that they can send copy down the line. You'll also make more of a professional impression if you invest in good quality headed paper and business cards.

• Learn to say no. It's easy to think, especially when you're starting out, that if you turn work down, you may never get offered any more. But you have to build in rest time and be careful of over-committing yourself: if you take on work when you're already busy, you could end up being unable to deliver on time or do the job as well as you could, which will put a client off using you again.

• Remember that journalism is all about contacts – the more people in the business you know, the more work you're going to get.

• Try not to get too dependent on one source of work. If the person who commissions or hires you leaves, you could suddenly find you're not used any more. A replacement will often bring in her own new pet freelances.

You have to be self-reliant and have the confidence to sell yourself and your work. You also need to be adaptable and flexible, able to fit in quickly with different people and different ways of working.

Remember that as a freelance you have no sick leave and no paid holidays, and bear that in mind when negotiating a rate of pay. What may initially seem a good hourly or daily rate may not be so attractive when you realize what its equivalent would be as an annual salary. To work it out, take the number of days in the year, 365, then deduct from that weekends (104), the number of days' paid holiday you would normally get (say, 25), eight days for statutory bank holidays, and, say, one week for sick leave. That brings you down to 223 earning days a year. So a daily rate of £100 a day is equivalent to a staff salary of around £22,300; an hourly rate of £12.15 (assuming a seven-hour working day) equates to around £19,000. That's assuming that you work every available day. In addition, you have to allow for the expense of all the things staff employees can take for granted – stationery, lighting, phone calls, heating, computer equipment, reference books, secretarial and admin support, pens and paper-clips.

Freelance Writing

Freelance writers have to be disciplined creatures, able to motivate themselves and work well in isolation. It is possible for them to make a good living but it is *not* an easy option. You constantly have to sell yourself, your skills and your ideas to editors, fit in with their, sometimes unreasonable, deadlines and chase them relentlessly for payment.

If you're commissioned to write something, make sure you get a clear brief – and, preferably, a written one. Try to work for places that pay on acceptance rather than on publication, otherwise you can find you've done all the work but have to wait months – sometimes even years – for the money.

Most newspapers and magazines do not welcome unsolicited manuscripts. It's better to send in cuttings and synopses of four or five *relevant* ideas rather than finished pieces. Alternatively, ring up and ask first whether or not they're interested in your ideas. Read at least a couple of copies of the publication you want to write for, so that you can get a feel for the sort of articles they use and the style in which they're written. It's surprising how many freelances waste time suggesting their ideas to inappropriate publications or programmes. Equally, there's no point sending a 10,000 word feature to a magazine that never runs anything longer than 1,200 words. And don't bother submitting material for slots that are supplied by regular columnists. If you insist on sending in an unsolicited manuscript, it's unlikely to be returned unless you enclose an sae.

When first starting out, you *must* be prepared to write 'on spec' – no one will commission you to write pieces until you've written successfully for them before. Try to contribute freelance articles to a local newspaper, student magazine or specialist trade publication; it's invaluable in terms of experience and also because it gets your name in print. After you have built up your portfolio of cuttings you will be in a much stronger position to approach features editors of larger publications.

All articles should be typed and double-spaced, on A4 paper (one side only) with adequate margins to both right and left of the text. Few people will bother to try to decipher pages of strange handwriting, or badly typed copy that runs the whole width of the page. Never send an original without keeping a copy, and don't send photographs or transparencies unless asked to do so.

Other Freelance Opportunities

The cutbacks in permanent staff numbers throughout the media mean increasing opportunities for freelances of all sorts: editors, producers, subs, proofreaders, researchers, commissioning editors, fashion stylists, designers, and many more are all busy freelancing.

Whereas freelance writers, editors and proofreaders work mostly from home, many other freelance jobs involve working 'on site' for a daily rate of pay. This is generally fixed within a company but is sometimes negotiable if you're particularly good (or they're particularly desperate!) or if you're committing to somewhere for a longer-than-normal period of time.

In publishing, average hourly rates, according to the Society of Freelance Editors and Proofreaders are £8.60 for proofreading and £10 for copy editing, although the NUJ recommends £12.15 and £13.25 respectively. In newspapers and magazines, daily rates for subs and designers are generally between £85 and £115, sometimes up to £140. Commissioning editors will probably get between £115 and £140 a day.

As every freelance will tell you, there are ups and downs to the freelance life: sometimes you'll be really glad you work for yourself; other times you'll crave the security of a staff job. Most, however, feel that the disadvantages are outweighed by the advantages – greater variety, more freedom, the chance to meet lots of new people and build up great contacts, being able to take your holidays when you choose, and flexibility to work round other commitments in your life.

Kate Lock

Age : **34**
Job : **Freelance writer/editor**
Based : **York**
Salary : **c. £24–28,000**
Qualifications : **BA (Hons.) Philosophy**

'I got interested in the media at university and after I left did reviews for a local paper, the *Oxford Star*, at £5 a time. When the arts editor left they gave me a couple of days' try-out; by the end of the week I had produced the entire leisure section of the paper with no prior experience so I got the job!

'After that I was assistant editor on a free London listings magazine for nine months before joining *Radio Times* as a sub-editor on the local radio desk. I was promoted on to features subs, then to deputy chief sub and then to promotions editor – a challenging experience but not really my cup of tea. After stress-related problems with my health, I ditched it to go freelance and I'm so glad I did.

'Now I'm writing for *Radio Times*, the *Yorkshire Post*, and the *Daily*

Telegraph, as well as editing for BBC Books. I start work each day by nine thirty to ten and carry on until one thirty (lunch and *Neighbours*). At two I'm back in my office, until five when my partner returns. We have a cup of tea and I go back to work until seven or seven thirty. I usually work weekends and often quite late into the evening. I'm trying to build in a keep-fit schedule because I've put on weight and I'm positive it's because I don't have to walk to work any more!

'Freelancing isn't just about getting jobs, it's also running a lot of equipment, being my accountant, being my own project manager. I'm finance, personnel, secretarial, editorial and systems support in one and it's hard work! Also, working from home means you don't get out much to meet people. We've been in York a year and I know the fishmonger, the newsagent and the grocer quite well but I don't have any girlfriends to gossip with!

'It isn't necessarily harder to get work outside London; if anything, there's less competition. But a lot of London editors do think that if you're beyond the M25 you're out of reach, even with a fax and modem. They still don't realize what you can do with the technology. We don't need to be in the capital. I think this way of working is the future – and, oh, how I love not being on the Tube!'

Charlotte Fadipe

Age : **31**
Job : **Freelance producer/reporter**
Based : **London**
Salary : **c. £30,000**
Qualifications : **B.Sc. (Hons.) Chemistry**

'I first got into the industry almost by accident when I was a student helping at a community centre. I went to the local radio station to publicize the work we were doing – and promptly fell in love with the media! After university I joined the BBC local radio journalist training scheme and spent two years working in various radio stations around the country. Then I joined BBC CWR in Coventry as a news producer, one of the youngest and the only black woman news producer at the time.

'I left in 1991 to go freelance, for the challenge and for better money and more excitement. Since then I've worked in TV (Channel 4, ITN, BBC, CNN, etc.) as a news reporter and producer. I also make corporate videos and training videos, and present for BBC World Service.

'As a freelance you can get a lot of experience and variety in a short amount of time, and it can be quite lucrative, depending on who you work for. But there are also many negative factors. The most obvious is the insecurity that comes with not having a regular pay packet. There is also a loss of status: people often assume that if you were good somebody would have employed you! You constantly have to sell yourself, which is very tiring, physically and mentally. There is also little career development – employers rarely encourage freelances to take on new responsibilities and you don't get access to company training courses. It's easy to work yourself to death and not take any holiday, just saying yes to whatever comes along. The reverse is also easy – just choosing what you want and then not having enough money to pay the mortgage. Self-discipline is vital to a freelance.

'It's hard sometimes to be seen just as someone to fill in the gaps when the company has a personnel shortage. When I get depressed, I think, "They don't see the whole me, they just see me as someone to fill up the newsroom rota." But then I cheer up by reminding myself that the company needs me, my skills, my talents, even if it is just for one day or one month. And, despite all the downsides, freelancing is fun.'

Chapter 6 / **Key Qualities**

In other chapters we've given an idea of the sort of qualities you need for specific jobs but there are certain core skills and abilities that are common to success in most areas of the media. When you ask any journalist about what they consider to be the keys to success, these are the points that crop up again and again.

• You need to be articulate with a good command of English (spoken and written), clear, concise writing skills and the ability to recognize good writing in others. You must also be able to visualize a story in print or on screen as well and have ideas for visuals to bring it alive.

• Commitment, enthusiasm and loads of stamina are vital – it's rare to find a journalistic job that's strictly nine-to-five and you need to be able to work long and irregular hours to tight deadlines.

• You'll have masses of ideas and the ability to recognize what makes a good story, what is relevant and what can be discarded; what makes news and what doesn't.

• You have to be able to get on with, and win the confidence of, all types of people. Interviewing skills call for a blend of persistence and tact, sympathy and scepticism.

• You need to have a healthy disrespect for figures of authority and all society's sacred cows, and should be quite unimpressed by fame or wealth. You should also be independent and impartial and above being swayed by freebies and bribes.

• You need to be good at making and maintaining contacts.

• You must have an eye for detail and be meticulous about accuracy and fact-checking. Any mistake makes your publication or programme look silly or ignorant; big mistakes can cost it lots of money.

• You need the ability to work quickly and efficiently under pressure and to make quick decisions. Understanding the importance of deadlines and being able to meet them, without panicking, is essential.

• You should have wide-ranging interests and a broad general knowledge, combined with an open mind and the ability to look at a story from all points of view and report it without bias – unless, of course, you're a columnist employed specifically for your strong opinions.

• Self-confidence, maturity, common sense and the ability to think logically will always stand you in good stead.

• You need plenty of motivation and initiative. In such a pressurized industry, no one has the time to nanny you so you must be able to spot what needs doing and when without being told.

• Persistence is a must. You have to be able to bounce back from rejection and not let it knock you off your stride. And you can have the most wonderful creative ideas in the world, but if you don't have the persistence to see them through, they'll just sit there. You must be able to take criticism of your work – a piece isn't published or broadcast until others have judged and commented on it.

• You need the willingness to put yourself on the line, determination to pursue a lead, plus natural curiosity and the desire always to get to the bottom of anything.

• The ability to work well as a member of a team is essential: most successful publications and programmes rely on good teamwork and there's no room for prima donnas.

• Nearly all journalists now work on screen so typing skills are essential and you must be computer literate. Apple Macs and PCs are widely used; Quark XPress and Microsoft Word are two of the most commonly found packages. Shorthand skills will always stand you in good stead, though many reporters prefer to use a tape recorder.

• Flexibility and a willingness to adapt and acquire new skills are important: in such a volatile world it's essential to futureproof yourself by continually updating your skills, keeping up with new technology and practices.

In such an increasingly competitive and cost-conscious world, would-be journalists must be aware that talent and creativity alone are often not enough. As the media become ever more business-like, employers now need people who are aware of market forces; who can come up with ideas on how to do things cheaper, faster, better; who understand the importance of meeting deadlines; who have ideas on how to increase sales and attract new readers/viewers/advertisers.

Chapter 7 / **How to Handle the Job Hunt**

Finding a job is always hard work – and as jobs in the media are even more coveted than most, a media job hunt is not for the faint of heart. You need vast reserves of resilience, persistence and determination. Even the most junior media role tends to attract hundreds of applicants so it could take some time – and a few rejections – before you finally strike it lucky.

First Steps

It's important to have a clear idea of which aspect of journalism will best suit you, so research the subject and read books to find out what job areas appeal.

The best way to find out what a particular job is really like is to talk to people who do it, so call people in your target area and ask if they would be prepared to chat to you for fifteen to twenty minutes about their work. The worst they can do is say no – but you may be pleasantly surprised by the number of people who'll be happy to spare you some time. Choose your time well when you ring and take the person's job into account: a magazine editor, for example, will probably have a pile of proofs to read late in the afternoon; the producer of a live show won't want to hear from you minutes before the programme goes on air. Make it clear that you're just looking for information and are not expecting to be offered a job. As well as asking them what their work involves, you could sound them out about the state of the industry, trends in the way things are going or what employers look for. Don't abuse their generosity: if you asked for fifteen minutes of their time, try not to take up more, unless they're obviously happy to carry on – and remember to send a thank-you letter soon after.

If your research reveals obvious gaps in your training or knowledge, do something about it, whether it's enrolling on a word-processing course or attending an industry conference. As well as improving your skills base, you'll also be providing an employer with a positive demonstration of your commitment and enthusiasm.

Make sure you *know* about the industry. Read the specialist press and the media pages of the newspapers (see Chapter 14) so that you're up to date on the issues affecting it. That way, you'll also know when companies are expanding or have won new contracts and might therefore be looking to recruit more staff.

If you're a student planning to break into the media after you leave university, you need to start gathering skills, practical experience and training as soon as possible to give you the edge over all the other thousands of graduates who'll be chasing jobs and postgraduate courses in the same narrow field. As well as the obvious things, like getting involved on the student newspaper or campus radio, make the most of any free training on offer, in computing or languages, for example, all of which can be useful skills in the media as well as in other jobs.

The one thing that will count for more than most is relevant work experience – and as much of it as possible – so good vacation jobs are vital. If you have secretarial skills, you may be able to find temping work. The other way of getting that all-important experience, and real insider view, is by offering to work for free. A good work placement will teach you more about the job than any careers book or counsellor can, and the experience gained can be more valuable than all the paper qualifications in the world when it comes to getting a permanent job. It's also a chance to make useful contacts and, if it goes well, will stand you in good stead when vacancies come up. *Cosmopolitan* has filled several junior positions by employing people who made a good impression on work experience. You're unlikely to be paid but some companies will cover your expenses – look on it as an investment.

Making the Most of Work Experience

• Lots of students look for work experience in the holidays, so you're more likely to get in if you can work during term-time. Apply at least a couple of months in advance, as it can be difficult to find a place.

• When you apply, state exactly what area of work you're interested in – fashion, research, reporting, etc. – and enclose a full CV. Give evidence of your interest, say what you hope to achieve and what they'll gain from having you.

• Be reliable. Even though you're not being paid a fortune – or, indeed, anything at all – you should behave professionally, arriving on time and not leaving before the end of the working day.

• Most of the work you're given will be thoroughly mundane (would *you* trust an inexperienced student with anything else?) but if you do the photocopying and tea-making with good grace you'll make a good impression. Do it with enthusiasm, or offer before asked, and you'll be remembered. However boring the tasks, do them all *well*: every little detail matters.

• It's always better to ask questions if you're doing something you don't understand than to blunder ahead and get it wrong. But whenever you ask a question, pay attention to the answer and write everything down so that you don't irritate people by asking the same things over and over again.

• Remember people's names: draw a plan of the office with names by desks to jog your memory.

• Try to move around departments to get a flavour of each, rather than staying at one desk the whole time.

• How you handle people on the phone will be noticed, so be polite, try to sound authoritative and make sure that when you take messages you get the contact's name and number right and note down the date and time. Watch how other people deal with callers. Don't take the opportunity of the 'free' phones to call all your friends. If you must make a personal call, ask permission first.

- Use your initiative. If someone looks really busy, offer to help; if the phone rings at an empty desk, answer it. Ask if there's any outstanding filing you could do or if the bookshelves need tidying. If there's really nothing, use the time to practise on the computer.
- If the placement was successful, ask someone with whom you worked closely if they would provide a reference for you. Try to get them to do it before you leave or soon after, before they forget who you are. If there's anyone you get on with particularly well, stay in contact with them and let them know you'd love to hear when any jobs are going.

Finding a Job

When it comes to journalism job ads, the tabloid media section of Monday's *Guardian* is far and away the best place to look, and you should make sure you read it every week. It's also worth trying *The Times* on Wednesdays (media, sales and marketing jobs, but mostly the latter) and the *Independent* on Tuesdays. The *Daily Mail*'s recruitment advertising section on Thursdays includes a section on Printing and Publishing and, in London, the *Evening Standard* on Wednesdays has a media section with some job ads. Those looking to come in via the secretarial route should head for La Crème de la Crème in *The Times* on Mondays, Wednesdays and Thursdays. The BBC publishes details of its current vacancies on CEEFAX p. 696. Many of the trade magazines carry recruitment advertising too – see Chapter 14 for details.

When you see a job ad that interests you, study it carefully. What sort of qualities and experience do you think the interviewer is looking for? How can you demonstrate that you have them? Don't be afraid to apply for a job just because you don't have every single quality asked for in the ad – employers know that the perfect candidate is a rare bird. As long as you meet most of the requirements, you're in with a chance.

However, sitting back and waiting for the perfect ad to appear in the paper could take years – so don't. Go out looking instead. It's been estimated that only 10 per cent of people find jobs by answering newspaper ads, and many employers try to cut costs and avoid a deluge of applications by relying on word of mouth to find suitable candidates. This is especially so in the media world, where many employers receive so many on spec applications or word-of-mouth recommendations that they rarely need to advertise jobs, especially at junior level.

Write directly to the person in charge of the department or programme, rather than to the personnel department, and specify the kind of work you're looking for. Your letter may then be passed on to Personnel but not before it's been seen by the person who really makes the decisions about whom to employ.

Networking is one of the best ways of finding a job, so increase your visibility and experience by attending relevant courses, industry conferences or talks. If anyone you know is employed in a company for which you want to work, ask them to keep an ear to the ground and an eye on the in-house notice-boards and magazines to find out if any jobs are going. Some companies offer a cash incentive to employees who can introduce new staff to the company and save them advertising the job.

Recruitment agencies are usually happier hunting grounds for secretaries and clerical workers, or for people working in media sales, than for journalists. However, one that specializes in journalism placements is the Media Network at 77 Oxford Street, London WIR IRB; (telephone 0171-437 0297), mostly used by publishers wishing to recruit at a more senior level. It does fill more junior positions too, but doesn't accept on its books anyone without relevant vocational training or experience.

The Perfect CV

The purpose of a CV is to get you an interview – and that applies whether you're writing to an employer on spec or applying for an advertised vacancy. The idea is to make it a tempting taster so that they'll want to find out more. It's not meant to tell the whole story of your life and should never be more than two sides long – no employer is going to want to read more than that. For recent graduates, one page is enough. Tailor your CV to each different job you apply for, emphasizing or downplaying different aspects as relevant. The fact that you spent several vacations working in catering may be of limited interest if you're applying for a job at a women's glossy magazine, but if you're being interviewed by a hotel and catering trade publication, it could provide relevant experience and knowledge of the industry. Remember to adapt your CV as the years go on, adding, cutting and rewriting. For example, the further away you get from your schooldays, the less relevant your O levels and GCSEs become, so prune back the details as more relevant experience supersedes them. Nor do you need to carry on putting down the holiday job you did when you were sixteen.

There are many different styles of CV and it's largely a question of taste as to which you choose. The traditional and most widely recognized follows a chronological format. After your basic personal details (name, address, telephone number, date of birth, nationality), give your career history, starting with your current or most recent job first, and working backwards. State the job title, company name, period of employment, give a brief job description and list any special achievements. Describe your current job in most detail; be more succinct about any before that. After Career History, list Educational Qualifications, again working backwards. You may also wish to include Other Information, such as driving licence, foreign languages, computer skills.

Alternatively, you could opt for a functional or skills CV. It's not as common but is useful if you have had frequent job changes, if you are trying to change career direction, or if you have a limited career history but have acquired relevant skills and experience in other areas, such as voluntary work or work experience. It also takes the emphasis off any gaps. Under headings such as Journalism Experience, Administrative Abilities or Communications Skills, summarize your experience in those areas. If you're applying for an advertised job, make sure you match your headings to the qualities asked for in the ad. Voluntary work is a particularly good source of transferable skills: teaching adult literacy or English as a second language calls for effective communication skills and an ability to motivate others; editing the student newspaper will probably have brought you experience in editing, writing, commissioning, researching and interviewing.

Your third option is a targeted CV, best used when you're applying for jobs on spec rather than in response to specific job advertisements. The emphasis is on aiming for a specific position and explaining why you're qualified for it. Under the heading Job Target state the position you're aiming for – for example, programme researcher. Then, under headings such as Capabilities and Achievements, list your skills and talents which relate to your prospective position and what you've done so far that shows you'd be able to perform in the job. Further headings should include Work Experience and Education, as on a chronological CV.

Whichever format you choose, there are certain basic rules to follow:

• Use good quality white or off-white paper. Avoid anything fancy or gimmicky.

• Make the layout as attractive and accessible as possible: use a clear, easy-to-read typeface and leave wide margins and spaces between sections.

• Avoid long sentences. An employer wants to see the key facts at a glance and won't be impressed by rambling prose. Keep phrases short, punchy and active, starting with a verb, for example 'developed new programme strand', 'improved copy flow system'.

You don't need to say 'I' every time – who else would you be talking about in your CV?

• Cut out anything inessential. You don't need to include addresses of employers or educational institutions. If you have a degree, it's not necessary to itemize every GCSE subject and grade.

• A CV should always be typed – and *well* typed. If you can't do it yourself or don't have access to a machine, get someone who can and does to do it for you.

• There's no need to include referees here, unless you have such stunningly good ones that it would impress an employer. Never give anyone's name as a referee without checking with them first.

• Check, double-check and triple-check your CV – then give it to a friend to check again. Any mistakes will count against you.

• Eliminate the negative. A CV is a selling document, not the place to advertise every exam you've ever failed or career setback you've faced.

• Don't include current salary details unless asked to do so. People will make certain assumptions about you and your worth if you give them specific figures and you could put yourself out of the running by earning too little or too much. Plenty of time to talk money later.

• Include interests and hobbies if you have little work experience as yet; otherwise, leave them off unless they demonstrate a skill or quality relevant to the job or are so unusual that they will intrigue the interviewer.

• If applying for jobs abroad, enclose a passport photograph of yourself – it's more common to do this in other European countries than it is here.

• If you're responding to a job advertisement, make sure that the skills you highlight in your CV match those specified in the ad.

• Extra skills such as computer literacy and foreign languages are valuable, but don't make them up to impress. If you claim to have fluent French, for example, you could find an interviewer asking you some questions in that language.

The Covering Letter

Never send off a CV or application form without a covering letter: it's a great opportunity to sell yourself. (If you have a glowing testimonial or letter of recommendation from a former employer, you could enclose that too.) Keep it short and to the point: it should fit on to one sheet, preferably on the same, high-quality paper as your CV.

Put your address in the top right-hand corner or centred at the top of the page, and the date and address of the person you're sending it to below that on the left-hand side. Make sure you address the letter to someone by name rather than 'The Personnel Officer' or 'Dear Sir/Madam'. Call the company first to find out, and always check the spelling. The correct ending to a letter addressed to a person by name is 'Yours sincerely'. 'Yours faithfully' is only used when the addressee is Dear Sir or Dear Madam.

Make sure the letter is tidy: if there are lots of applicants for a job, it's easy to start by discarding the ones whose replies are scruffy or ill-prepared. Typing looks smarter, unless the employer specifically requests a handwritten letter, in which case draft it on a rough piece of paper first so that you can write the final letter without mistakes. Use blue or, preferably, black ink; other colours are generally frowned upon and green ink is considered the trademark of a loony.

With any job application, it's important that your spelling, grammar and punctuation are correct. If you're applying for a job in journalism, it's *doubly* important. Any applicant for a sub-editor's position who makes a spelling mistake in her letter definitely won't be asked for an interview.

If you're applying for a specific job, say how you heard about it, and if there is a reference number, include it. If you're writing at the suggestion of someone the employer knows personally or someone who is well known in the field, then mention it straight away. Keep the language simple: many people make the mistake of using over-formal, flowery phrases, which sound stilted and unnatural. State briefly why you are a strong candidate and emphasize what you have to offer the employer: 'As music editor of the university newspaper, I have had plenty of experience in dealing with PRs and celebrities, interviewing and writing, and have acquired a number of valuable contacts.' It is not good enough to say, 'I'd love to work in the media.' So would a million others. Draw attention to the relevant bits of your CV but don't go into details. Save that for the interview.

Don't write a fabulous letter, then ruin the effect by cramming it into a tiny little envelope. Your paper should never be folded more than twice, so make sure your envelope is A4, A5, or 220 × 110mm.

Application Forms

Many companies, especially large organizations such as the BBC, ask all applicants to fill in an application form, rather than sending in a CV. It makes it easier for them to find the information they need to know quickly, which is invaluable when dealing with large numbers of candidates.

Photocopy the blank form and do a rough version of your answers on the photocopy first, then, once you're happy with it, copy them on to the original. Complete all sections, however irrelevant they might seem. Don't leave the Further Information box blank – if you do, you'll miss a chance to shine and mention things you haven't had the opportunity to put in elsewhere. Look back at the job ad to see what they were asking for and if you haven't managed to prove how well you match the description anywhere else, now's your chance. Write legibly and in black ink: the form will probably be photocopied and blue ink doesn't photocopy well.

Take a photocopy of the finished form as a useful reference for the next time you have to fill one in.

Interviews

Interviews can be nerve-racking, especially for first-time jobhunters – and the more you want the job, the worse it is. The more you plan ahead, though, the better your chances and the better you'll feel on the day. Research may be time-consuming but it's worth it: it shows initiative and motivation and will give you a great advantage over candidates who haven't bothered. If you're ignorant about the company's work, then you're obviously not that interested in them or, presumably, the job. Don't be careless: confusing the company's products with those of a rival won't win you any friends.

You should already be reading the relevant trade press (see Chapter 14) to keep up to date on the industry generally. If you're going for a job on a newspaper or magazine, read as many issues of the publication as possible so that you know it backwards. What features or articles did you particularly enjoy? Which writers do you admire? What readership is it aiming at? What changes would you make to the content or design? Read rival publications, too, so that you can make knowledgeable comparisons and comments.

If you're applying for a job in TV or radio, follow the same rules. Watch or listen to the programme. What do you particularly like/dislike about it? What sort of contribution have different members of the team made? Would you have handled certain things differently and, if so, how? How aware are you of other programmes in the same field?

For book publishing, you should make sure that you get a copy of the publisher's catalogue to see what recent titles it has published and what authors are on its books. Which do you particularly admire? What areas does the publisher specialize in? What do you think of the jacket designs and typefaces, etc? Spend a day browsing in a bookshop watching how books are displayed and what people are buying.

Whatever the job you're going for, the following tips apply.

• Expect to be asked about your personal life and leisure interests as well as strictly work issues. The employer is trying to put together a picture of you as a complete person.

• If you're working already, prepare a clear, succinct précis of your job and be prepared to answer questions on any aspect of it. Past performance is the main thing employers have to rely on when it comes to assessing how well you would do with them so make sure you feed them relevant examples of your experience. How have you shown initiative, reliability, creativity, organizational flair? Can you work well under pressure or adapt to changing conditions? What computer systems can you use?

• Be ready to explain why you're interested in this job. Sounds obvious, yes, but it's surprising how many people don't think it through.

• Be prepared for tests. Subs, for example, may be given a mistake-ridden proof with lots of overmatter and asked to correct it, cut it to fit and write captions, headline and intros. Sometimes there will be a general-knowledge or current-affairs test so make sure you're up to date with the news (if you're applying for work in a newsroom, this should go without saying).

• Straightforward questions about your studies, qualifications or job history are relatively easy to answer and you should certainly expect to be asked any of the questions in the box below. Many media interviews are relatively informal chats but there are always some interviewers who like to spring on you horrors such as 'How would your best friend/worst enemy/colleagues describe you?' or 'What are your strengths/weaknesses?' You're unlikely to think of something suitable on the spot so it helps to think ahead and have examples prepared. *Great Answers to Tough Interview Questions* by Martin John Yate (Kogan Page £6.99), has some great tips on how to answer potential clangers.

Questions You're Likely to be Asked

Tell me about yourself.

What makes you right for this job?

Why do you want to work for us?

What do you like/dislike in your current job?

Why do you want to leave your current job?

Where do you see yourself·in five years' time?

Tell me all about your current job.

What do you think of the magazine/paper/programme/catalogue; what are your favourite bits; what would you change?

What computer systems have you worked on?

How do you feel about working long hours?

• If you're going for your first job after school or university, you're unlikely to have much work experience, so you'll have to look to other areas for skills and experience to offer employers. Did you participate in team sports? Write for the school magazine? Make short films with the film society? Take leading roles in school plays? Serve on a hall of residence committee? Deliver seminars? Undertake extensive or unusual travel during vacations? Have you done voluntary work, served time on a local community committee or been involved in an advisory board? Have you had any work placements during the holidays? Be prepared to answer questions about why you did these things and what you feel you've gained from them. Even things that seem irrelevant to you may help to give an employer a fuller picture of you.

• As much as anything, employers want evidence that you are reliable and responsible so even non-media-related work experience at weekends or in vacations could illustrate those qualities. If you've paid for any postgraduate studies yourself, it shows strong motivation and commitment so make sure you mention it. If you're a bit rusty at interviews try to run the whole thing through with a more practised friend beforehand, getting her to play the interviewer – she may come up with more possible questions you hadn't thought of. You may feel silly at first but it *will* help. Ask for honest feedback and don't get upset or defensive if there are negative points, as that will just discourage further comment. Don't over-rehearse or you'll end up sounding stilted and unnatural when you want to appear spontaneous and relaxed.

• You don't always get much notice of an interview so don't leave all your preparation until the letter arrives. Start thinking about it when you do your application.

• Don't spend so long worrying about the questions you'll be asked that you forget the basics. Get plenty of sleep the night before the interview. Work out in advance how you're going to get there and how long it will take, and allow extra time for delays. A couple of days ahead make sure that your clothes are clean and ready.

On the Day

Getting in the Mood

• Be positive! If you've been asked for an interview, they're obviously interested in you. To get to this stage you've probably already beaten hundreds of others and may be on a short list of between six and twelve. The employer already believes you are *capable* of the job; all you have to do is prove it.

• Do anything to help boost your confidence: read a favourite poem or inspirational book on the way to the interview, listen to 'up' music on your Walkman, remind yourself of all the times you've triumphed against the odds or all the things you've done that make you feel proud.

• Reread your letter/CV/application form and be ready to answer questions on anything you've included. Take copies with you in case the interviewer has mislaid them.

• Take a spare pair of tights, needle and cotton (for emergency repairs), phonecard and small change, (for parking or phone calls). Make sure you have the company's phone number so you can call in an emergency. And don't forget to take their address.

• Set out in plenty of time and aim to arrive 10–15 minutes early. Don't expect buses or trains to turn up on time or assume that you'll find a parking space easily. Use your waiting time to watch the people around you, read any internal notice-boards or in-house newsletters, and generally try to get a feel for the place.

• Don't smoke or drink shortly before the interview. Smelling of smoke or alcohol isn't going to impress any interviewer.

Looking the Part

Don't underestimate the importance of appearance. Research has shown that an interviewer's impression of you will be made up of 55 per cent how you look, 38 per cent on how you sound and only 7 per cent on what you say. First impressions are quickly formed and hard to change, and although your interview might last an hour, a decision has probably been largely made within the first four or five minutes.

• Your clothes don't need to be expensive – nobody expects some-one fresh out of college to waltz in in Armani – but they must be presentable and clean. Make sure they're comfortable, too: you can't concentrate on the interview if you're too busy worrying about wayward buttons or squirming around because your skirt's too tight.

• Dress appropriately for the organization: you wouldn't necessarily wear the same outfit for a BBC interview as you would for a job at Planet 24, for example. As a general rule, though, think smart rather than trendy. Some experts recommend going to watch staff leaving or entering the workplace, so you can get an idea of the corporate image and tailor your interview outfit accordingly (same kind of clothes but a bit smarter).

• Heels look smarter than flat – but not *too* high – and studies suggest that wearing light, natural make-up rather than none at all increases your chances of success by 20 per cent.

• Don't smoke, even if invited to do so – it looks messy. And, unless you're ultra-relaxed, refuse any offers of tea or coffee as well – they just provide more scope for disaster.

• Don't go into the interview room clutching carrier bags of shopping or a dripping wet coat and umbrella; leave any encumbrances with the receptionist to look after.

• Try to appear confident, even if you're quaking inside. Walk in confidently and sit upright but relaxed in the chair. Leaning slightly forward shows attention and interest. Look the interviewer in the eye but don't fix her with an unwavering stare. Speak up and, if you tend to gabble when nervous, make a conscious effort to speak more slowly. Try to sound enthusiastic. Keep your arms and legs uncrossed, don't shift around in your seat and try not to fiddle with jewellery or your hair. Merely sitting comfortably gives you the desired impression of calm and confidence.

• However nervous you feel, *smile*! Most interviewers base their final decisions on gut feeling, and it's only natural that they will warm more to someone who appears relaxed and friendly, someone they think will be pleasant to work with as well as able to do the job.

• Don't save your best behaviour for the interviewer alone: be just as pleasant to the receptionist and anyone else you make contact with – they may be asked for their impressions.

In the Interview

• If the interviewer starts by asking you a few general questions like how your journey to the interview was, she's only trying to put you at your ease – don't go into great detail.

• A bit of humour or wit at appropriate moments will make you more memorable to an interviewer and provide a bit of light relief in what is, for her, probably a rather dull day of grilling nervous candidates.

• Concentrate on listening properly to what the interviewer is saying rather than fretting about how you're doing and what she might ask next. If you miss something or are confused by a question, it's better to ask for clarification than to waffle on with an inappropriate answer. Keep your answers relevant.

• It's normal to play up your good points and try to skim over the bad ones, but you don't want to look as if you have something to hide. If the interviewer asks about any area you'd hoped to avoid – a previous redundancy, say, or a series of short-term jobs – answer briefly but honestly.

• If you're asked why you want to leave your current job, don't just say you're bored or hate your boss, even if it's true. Couch your reasons in more positive terms: 'I've learned a great deal in the job but now I've reached a stage where there are no immediate promotion prospects and I'm ready to tackle new challenges/take on more responsibility/use talents that are underused at the moment.'

• Be specific in your answers. If you're asked how you would handle situation X, for example, tell the interviewer, if you can, how you dealt successfully with a similar situation in the past. Otherwise admit your ignorance and try to come up with a possible solution.

• Employers usually take up references so don't lie about something a referee might be asked to corroborate.

• Panel or board interviews, as used by the BBC, for example, can be especially daunting but at least you're less at the whim of one person's likes and dislikes. Sit somewhere where you can see everyone and they can all see you – if the chair's in the wrong place, move it. Members of a panel usually take it in turns to ask questions and you should watch the questioner as she talks to you, then address your answers mainly to her, but include the other panel members with occasional eye contact. Return your gaze to the chairperson at the end. If possible, find out in advance who the members of the panel will be. Try to memorize the names and to be equally polite and friendly to all members, whatever their manner. When you get your turn to ask questions, direct them to the chair, who can then redirect them to the appropriate member of the panel.

• If there's a silence after you've given your answer to a question, don't feel you have to blunder in and fill it. Just ask the interviewer if you've made yourself clear and put the ball firmly back in her court.

• If you're asked about your hobbies and interests, don't say anything you can't back up. If you say you're keen on the theatre, for example, expect to be asked, 'What is the best play you've seen recently?'

• Remember, this is a two-way process: it's a time for you to find out about the potential employer and the job as well as vice versa, so don't miss your chance when asked if you have any questions. It also provides another opportunity for you to impress. Prepare three or four intelligent questions that demonstrate your genuine interest in the job or your familiarity with the business and the challenges facing it. Write them down on an index card if you think you might forget them and keep it conveniently to hand. If the interviewer doesn't offer you the chance to ask questions, then volunteer, but remember that asking too many is as bad as asking none at all. Be sensitive about time and alert to signs of impatience in the interviewer – remember that the next candidate is probably waiting. If all your questions have been answered during the course of the interview, then say so.

- Questions about childcare and marital status are illegal but that doesn't stop some people asking them. If you want the job, it's probably best just to deal with them briefly but assure the interviewer that you can cope and wouldn't have applied for the job otherwise.
- Don't leave the interview without asking how soon you can expect to hear from them.

Money Matters

Many people will just accept whatever money is offered in their relief at getting the job, but salary is almost always open to negotiation, providing you go about it in the right way.

Before you go to an interview, try to find out the going rate for the job. Ask people working in the industry; contact professional associations; look at similar job ads to see if they mention money.

If you're asked how much you earn now, remember to take into account any perks you may have, such as subsidized canteen, pension, profit share, interest-free travel loan or medical insurance. Always try to get the employer to mention a figure before you do but if they ask you to say what you're looking for, don't think in terms of what you need but in terms of what the job is worth. Don't give a fixed figure, but a range: 'I'm looking for something in the high twenties' or 'I would hope for a substantial increase on the £12,000 I'm earning now.' If they give a range, aim for the top.

If the employer is immovable on the money, or won't go as high as you'd like, think about other areas that might be open to negotiation, such as flexible working hours, an early salary appraisal, training opportunities, or a company car.

After the Interview

Assess your performance and see if there's anything you can learn from it. What went well? What went badly? If there were any questions that caught you out, brush up your answers for next time. If, despite all your best efforts, the interview was a disaster, don't automatically blame yourself. If you're unlucky enough to land an unpleasant or aggressive interviewer, you'll just have to write it off to experience and remind yourself that the next one can only be better.

However the interview went, it's a good idea to write the next day, thanking the interviewer for seeing you, reinforcing any important points and adding any extra relevant information you might have forgotten or been unable to pass on at the time. Keep it short and sweet – just enough to nudge the interviewer's memory and show that you really are keen. If you don't hear anything within the time expected, write or call to find out the state of play. Let them know if you have other interviews or offers to consider but don't make it sound like a threat. After the initial inquiry, leave it – hassling only irritates people.

If you're offered the job, clarify all terms and conditions before accepting. If you wait until you're in the job before sorting things out, you're in a weaker position to bargain. Don't hand in your notice in your current job until you have something in writing from your new employer: a verbal offer can be withdrawn.

If you don't get the job but you're still keen to work for the company, write and say you were sorry to be unsuccessful this time but would like to be kept on file in case of future vacancies. It wouldn't hurt to ask what the person who was appointed had that you didn't. Make it clear you're just looking for helpful feedback and not demanding an explanation. At least it might give you something useful to take away from the experience rather than seeing it as a total failure.

Keeping up morale is important. It can be discouraging when you apply unsuccessfully time and time again, especially when your friends are all finding their dream jobs, but don't let yourself sink into depression. Treat each interview as practice and remember that if you take great care over your letters and CVs you're already streets ahead of most people. Your time will come.

Chapter 8 / **Guide to Jargon**

Like all industries, the media world has a language of its own, which can leave you wondering what they're all talking about when you first start. It's made even more confusing in that different companies have their own jargon: for example, 'titles' on one magazine may become 'headlines' on another, or 'intros' become 'standfirsts'. Here's a basic guide to mediaspeak for beginners, along with explanations of commonly used acronyms.

ABC   Audit Bureau of Circulation. ABC figures record the circulations of newspapers and magazines. For newspapers they are issued monthly, for magazines twice a year.

actuality   Interviews and background sounds recorded at a location outside the studio and used to give colour to a broadcast report.

advance   Sum paid upfront to an author writing a book. Usually paid in thirds: on signing the contract, on delivery of the manuscript and on publication. Called an advance because it is merely an advance payment of royalties and no more royalties are paid until the amount of the advance has been earned.

AI   Appreciation Index, or means of measuring how much viewers have *enjoyed* a programme, regardless of high or low viewing figures.

all rights   If a company buys all rights on a feature, it means they own copyright in it and can use it as often as they wish and do whatever they like with it, including sell it elsewhere.

angle   Slant that's put on a story to make it different (e.g. a new angle, a local angle, the woman's angle) or the particular aspect of it you pick up on.

back bench   Refers to senior editorial executives on a newspaper, responsible for overseeing its production.

banner headline   Large one that runs across the top of a page.

BARB Broadcasters' Audience Research Board: runs the world's largest audience monitoring system, tracing national viewing patterns.

body copy The main read of an article as distinguished from captions, headlines, boxed-out copy, sidebars (*q.v.*), etc.

BOT Black print on a tinted background.

brief A commissioning editor's description of what she wants a writer/reporter to do, how to tackle a story, etc. May be given in writing, over the phone or via a ten-second conversation in the office.

broadsheet Newspaper size used by quality press such as *The Times*, *Telegraph* and *Guardian*; often used as synonym for the quality press.

BSME British Society of Magazine Editors: arranges lunches, conferences, awards.

bullet points Short phrases, sentences, preceded by a blob: • .

byline Writer's credit on a piece. If accompanied by a headshot of the writer, known as a picture byline.

caps Capital letters.

cart Cartridge: an enclosed tape loop, carrying items, inserts or jingles for a programme.

casting off Involves estimating how much space a story or complete book manuscript would take up in a given type, point size (*q.v.*) and column width.

catchline Identifying heading given to a story by a reporter; usually just one key word.

chromalin Colour proof of full colour pages.

circulation Number of sales per issue of a newspaper or magazine, as distinct from readership.

copy The text produced by a writer.

copy flow Internal movement of copy round a magazine or newspaper.

credits On-screen or in-print mentions of people who have worked on a piece or programme.

crossheads Device used to break up text, consisting of a couple of words lifted from the text but not necessarily heralding the start of a new section. See also Subhead.

cutout Picture where the object or person has been cut away from the background to be silhouetted against white space.

DAB Digital Audio Broadcasting: a new high quality system of radio transmission.

deadline Date or time by which your job *must* be done.

DPS See Spread.

drop cap Initial letter that is larger than and dropped into the rest of the body copy.

dubbing Rerecording sound or pictures from one tape to another.

dummy Can be a mock-up of a proposed new publication to give prospective investors and advertisers an idea of what it will look like. Also used to describe a day-by-day assembly of proofs so that staff can see what stage the publication they're currently working on is at; it is sent to the printers at the end so they can check the f nal order of pages.

EFP Electronic field production; see ENG.

ENG Electronic news gathering, that is, filming with portable video camera rather than shooting on film. Also known as PSC (portable single camera) or EFP.

extent Number of pages in a publication.

facilities house Company providing specialized editing facilities for broadcasters, with edit suites, operators and editors.

FBSR First British Serial Rights: allows a publication to reproduce material for the first time and publish it in the UK and in one issue only, and often within a specified time.

flat plan Chart of how a magazine is going to be planned, showing order of contents, with both editorial and advertising pages. Each double-page spread is represented by a small rectangle divided in two. Kept on the office wall so everyone can see at a glance where in the magazine a feature falls.

fold To fold a publication is to close it down.

folio Page number.

font, fount Today, all the characters of a particular typeface.

full bleed When a picture runs right to the edge of the paper with no white space around.

full out When a line runs right across the full column, with no indentation either end.

galley   At one stage, the first proof after copy had been typeset. A galley proof shows straight columns of text, not fitted to a layout, and is cheaper to correct than the next stage, page proofs. Electronic page make-up has reduced the need for galley proofs.

gallery   Control room where director, PA and other staff sit during recording, issuing instructions to floor staff.

glossies   Shorthand for upmarket women's magazines on quality glossy paper – *Cosmopolitan*, *Vogue*, etc.

green room   Hospitality room where guests wait before appearing on a programme.

gutter   The channel down the centre of a double-page spread.

house   Publishing firm.

house style   Set of rules (covering spelling, abbreviations, punctuation, etc.) whose aim is to ensure consistency throughout a publication; for example, house style dictates whether to use Peking or Beijing, 1st September or September 1, MP or M.P., Managing Director or managing director, organise or organize?

intro   In newspapers, the opening paragraph of a story, containing the gist of the story. For magazines, see Standfirst.

ISBN   International Standard Book Numbering.

JICREG   Joint Industry Committee for Regional Press Research. Provides limited readership information for the regional press.

kerning   Increasing or reducing the spacing between letters or words.

kill   To kill a story is to ditch it. A writer whose story is killed is usually paid a kill fee, a percentage, which varies, of the original fee agreed for the piece.

layout   The design of a page.

leader   Newspaper opinion piece, related to a topical issue and voicing the general attitude of the paper's editor and readers.

leading   Amount of white space between lines of text – if text is cramped and hard to read, increasing the leading can help; reducing it would help fit in something that might be too long.

masthead   In magazines, the list of staff's names and job titles printed inside; on newspapers, refers to the title logo on the front page.

monkey Fleet Street slang for a photographer.

MTA Minimum Terms Agreement: the minimum a publisher can offer an author.

NBA Net Book Agreement (now abandoned; see p. 78).

nib Short for news in brief, or short news paragraphs.

NRS National Readership Survey: monitors average issue readership of newspapers and magazines, frequency and quality of reading, provides readership data for newspapers and magazines.

OB Outside broadcast, or programme being transmitted from outside the studio.

on spec On-spec copy is copy that is sent in to a publication without them having requested it. If someone asks you to send copy in on spec, it means they will read it but are making no promises about buying it and have not agreed to commission you.

orphan First line of a paragraph at the bottom of a page or column. Also called a club line. See also Widow.

overmatter Text that overruns the space allowed on a layout – the copy would have to be cut back to fit it in.

package Finished broadcast report, complete with interviews and links, ready to go. Broadcast equivalent of a feature.

page proofs Text made up into pages with folios, heads and subheads, picture captions, etc.

pagination Number of pages in a given issue of a newspaper or magazine.

panel See Sidebar.

peg Something that provides the justification for running a story, for example, a food feature on treacle toffee and parkin for which the peg would be Bonfire Night.

perfect bound Sealed with glue as opposed to any other form of binding, e.g. staples.

point size Unit for measuring size of typeface.

POV Point Of View.

PPA Periodical Publishers Association.

proof Representation of layout, text, pictures, headlines, etc. for checking and correction (see Galley, Page proofs).

PSC Portable Single Camera (see ENG).

pull-out quote   Quote taken from text and displayed in larger type.

RAJAR   Radio Joint Audience Research: measures audience listening figures for commercial and BBC radio stations.

ranged left/right   Start or end of every line is aligned on left or right side of text, while other side is ragged, or unaligned.

raw copy   Copy as received direct from a writer, before it's gone through the subbing process.

readership   Number of people estimated to read, as opposed to buy, each issue of a newspaper or magazine.

remaindering   Practice of selling off books cheap when they fail to move at full price.

rip and read   Wire service (*q.v.*) stories that can be ripped off the printer and read on air.

royalties   The percentage of the cover price of a book paid to the author; usually between 7 and 10 per cent on paperbacks, 10 to 15 per cent on hardbacks.

R/T   Running time, or length of programme.

rules   Borders, lines.

rushes   Unedited tapes or print.

scanner   Large van housing a mobile control room, used for OBs (*q.v.*) – can put package together on location and beam back to the station.

screamer   Exclamation mark.

sell   Another word for standfirst (*q.v.*) (also known as intro).

sexy   Used to describe any story that will have great viewer/listener/reader appeal.

sidebar   Panel of text accompanying the main read.

slug   Can mean same as catchline; also used to describe identifying subtitle that appears on regular features, e.g. 'food', 'living', 'horoscopes', etc.

soundbyte   The part of an interview that is broadcast.

spike   A spiked story is one that doesn't get used.

spread   Two facing pages; also called a DPS or double-page spread.

standfirst   Introduction to a story (also known as a sell or intro).

storyboard   Rough up of a television storyline, in the form of a cartoon strip.

strapline   Secondary headline appearing above and expanding on the main headline.

subhead   Subheading that serves to break up text and help make it easier to read; unlike a crosshead, it usually marks a new section of text.

tabloid   Size of newspapers such as the *Sun, Daily Express, Daily Mail*, half the size of a broadsheet; used as a synonym for the downmarket papers.

text   See Body text.

think piece   Longer, more in-depth piece on a given theme.

tip-off   Suggestion about a possible story, something worth checking out.

titles   See Headline.

TOT   Stands for 'triumph over tragedy'; term used for heart-rending human-interest stores.

tranny   Short for transparency.

turn   Continuation page of a feature.

TX   Transmission; TX 9 March, for example, means the programme will be broadcast on that date.

typeface   Design of type.

typo   Short for typographic error, which is one made in typing or typesetting.

UHER   Portable reel-to-reel tape recorder.

VO   Voice-over or commentary added to pictures.

vox pop   From Latin *vox populi*, voice of the people; term used when interviewers go out on the street to get a range of viewpoints on a subject from a cross-section of the public.

VT   Video tape.

VTR   Video Tape Recorder.

well   Series of editorial spreads uninterrupted by advertising, usually used in women's magazines for fashion pages and big features.

widow   Short last line of a paragraph on its own at the top of a page or column, which is generally frowned upon. See also Orphan.

wire services   Agencies who gather news from around the world and send it to subscribers.

WOB   White On Black, that is, white type on a black background.

Main Proofreading/Subbing Marks

When reading and correcting proofs, proofreaders use a special set of marks, a few of which are described below. The position of a correction is marked in the text but the correction itself is marked in the margin. Subs and copy-editors can edit straight on to the text, but may use proofreading marks for clarification.

Anything ringed is an instruction and not something to be inserted.

• To mark the end of a correction in the margin, do an oblique stroke /.

• To delete something, put a line through the copy to go and mark ⌒ in the margin (it's a Greek *d* joined to a concluding mark (see above)).

• To reinstate something you have mistakenly crossed out, draw a dotted line under the copy to be reinstated and write *stet* (ringed) in the margin.

• To add new copy, do an insertion mark ⋏ at the point you want it to go in, then write the addition in the margin, followed by a concluding mark.

• If you want to change the type to italic, draw a straight line under the relevant words and write *ital* (ringed) in the margin. For bold, do a wavy line and write *bold* (ringed) in the margin. For roman, put a ring round the words and write *rom* (ringed) in the margin.

• If you want copy putting in capital letters, draw three straight lines underneath and write *caps* (ringed) in the margin.

• To close up a gap between words or letters, do ⌒ linking the two sides and repeat the mark in the margin (or write *c/u* (ringed)).

- To insert more space, use an insertion mark (see above) and write # in the margin.
- To transpose words or letters in the wrong order, do a transposition mark ⊔⊓ (e.g. ⌊order⌈wrong⌋) and write *trs* (ringed) in the margin.
- Mark [or ⌐ on the copy to indicate the start of a new paragraph, with *np* (ringed) in the margin. If you want to run two paragraphs together, draw a line linking the end of one to the start of the next ⌒ and write *r/o* (ringed) in the margin.

Chapter 9 / **Education and Qualifications**

The NUJ specifies a minimum educational qualification for people entering newspaper journalism of five GCSEs, including English language. However, it is rare now to find anyone, in any branch of the media, starting out at this level. More and more entrants to all areas of journalism have a degree or equivalent qualification, and many who aren't graduates will have at least a couple of A levels. Two A levels or equivalent is also the minimum entry qualification for most higher education courses.

Whatever level you enter at, you will be expected to have a high standard of competence in the English language but that doesn't mean that your degree has to be in media studies, English or journalism. Depending on what field you go into, there are plenty of other subjects that can be just as relevant to your career, if not more so. A background in politics, history and economics, for example, would come in handy on a news desk; science graduates who can convey technical information in a lively, accessible form are always sought after; and as we become more closely integrated into Europe, languages are increasingly in demand.

However, the number of specifically media-related courses available at undergraduate and postgraduate level is increasing all the time and we've included details of some of those currently available under 'Higher Education'. Industry bodies such as the NUJ, NCTJ, PTC and NCTBJ (see Chapter 10) will provide lists of courses approved by them and you can assume that these are generally well received by employers. (Taking one of the industry-endorsed courses may have added benefits such as free temporary membership of the relevant union.) ITV can also supply a list of those courses they think are worthwhile, but they stress that completing such a course does not, of course, guarantee a job at the end.

Competition for the most popular courses can be every bit as intense as it is for jobs. The Cardiff Centre for Journalism Studies, for example, reports over 500 applications a year for thirty places on its Newspaper Option; LCP has around 1,000 applications for the thirty-four places on its BA in Media Studies. Overall, applications for media studies courses increased by 54 per cent in 1995 – up to nearly 33,000 from just over 21,000 the year before. Give plenty of time and attention to your application, just as you would for a job interview. Probably around half of those who initially apply are rejected; the rest are set a task to do (say, a 500-word essay on why you want to be a journalist or a critique of a recent radio programme), and of these, probably another half are lost. See Chapter 7 for some idea of the sort of qualities they'll be looking for in a successful candidate and Chapter 8 for general job-hunting advice that will stand you in good stead for a college interview too. Admissions tests may set such tasks as constructing a news story from some given facts; correcting sentences containing grammatical errors or spelling mistakes; and answering general-knowledge questions.

Check out a course carefully before you apply, because the content – especially the amount of practical work – varies greatly. Some courses are more theoretical and academic so get hold of a prospectus or talk to tutors, and find out how well a course suits your needs. How much practical experience will you get? How much individual attention? Is a work placement included as part of the course and will the college organize it for you? What sort of equipment does the department have and how much use can you make of it? How much job-finding help will you be given? Does the college or university have its own radio station, newspaper or studios on which you can gain practical work experience? Find out what previous students have gone on to do; see if you can talk to current students about the course. What experience do the tutors and lecturers have?

NVQs/SVQs

Gradually being adopted by media employers, National Vocational Qualifications (or SVQs in Scotland) are work-based qualifications that prove you can *do* a job, regardless of how you acquired your experience. You are assessed in the workplace and there is no specified form of training or time limit by which it must be completed. You just have to prove you can do (and have done), the job to the standards drawn up by industry bodies such as the PTC, Newspaper Society and Book House.

There are five levels of NVQ, from basic work activities (Level 1) to senior management (Level 5). Each level is broken down into a number of 'units of competence'. Unit 1 of the news-reporting NVQ, for example, is 'Generating story leads: writing'. This in turn is broken down into elements, in this case, 'Establish and maintain contact with information sources. Make routine inquiries. Identify potential stories.' You don't have to work your way through from Level 1 to 5 but can start wherever you and your employer feel is appropriate.

There are three NVQs in newspaper journalism (writing, production and press photography) and five in periodical journalism (news reporting, feature writing, subbing, subbing and layout, and magazine design). In book publishing, there are NVQs in editing, production, commissioning, design, publicity and promotion, publishing rights, publishing contracts, journal editing and production, and journal management and programme development. Skillset, the broadcast, film and video industry training body, is also starting to develop NVQs and SVQs in multimedia.

NVQs and SVQs are administered and awarded by bodies such as BTEC, SCOTVEC, City & Guilds, RSA and Open University, and will eventually replace some of their old-style vocational qualifications. For details of their current media-related courses, including those at pre-degree level which are not covered by this book, contact the awarding bodies direct.

BTEC (The Business & Technology
Education Council)
Central House, Upper Woburn Place,
London WC1H 0HH
Telephone: 0171 413 8400

SCOTVEC (Scottish Vocational
Education Council)
Hanover House, 24 Douglas Street,
Glasgow G2 7NG
Telephone: 0141 248 7900

City and Guilds of London Institute
1 Giltspur Street, London EC1A 9DD
Telephone: 0171 294 2468

**National Council for Vocational
Qualifications**
222 Euston Road, London NW1 2BZ
Telephone: 0171 728 1914

Oversees the formulation of NVQs in
different sectors and the assessments
provided by the various awarding
bodies.

**Open University Validation
Services**
344–354 Gray's Inn Road, London
WC1X 8BP
Telephone: 0171 278 4411
Has taken over from the Publishing
Qualifications Board in developing
NVQs in book publishing. Contact
Rosie Thom (Programme Manager,
Publishing) for details.

RSA Examinations Board
Westwood Way, Coventry CV4 8HS
Telephone: 01203 470033

Higher Education Courses

We have concentrated here on largely journalism-related courses.
For details of design-based courses or those concentrating on the
production/technical side (of which there are many, many more),
see *Media Courses UK*, edited by Lavinia Orton and published annually by the British Film Institute.

As a general rule, first degree courses last three years full time
(or four years in Scotland) and HND courses two years. Most
postgraduate, pre-entry and foundation courses are one year full
time. Occasionally courses may be longer, or shorter, or may be
available part time.

Barnsley College
Church Street, Barnsley, South
Yorkshire S70 2AX
Telephone: 01226 730191
BA (Hons.) Combined Studies

(Journalism) (emphasis on print
media); BA (Hons.) Combined Studies
(Media) (emphasis on broadcast
media); HND Media (Journalism).

Bell College of Technology
Almada Street, Hamilton, Lanarkshire
ML3 0JB
Telephone: 01698 283100
HND in Communication; HND in
Journalism; Postgraduate Diploma in
Radio Journalism.

The University of Birmingham
Edgbaston, Birmingham B15 2TT
Telephone: 0121 414 3344/3374
B.Soc.Si (Hons.) in Media, Culture and
Society; Media & Cultural Studies is
also offered as half of a BA Combined
Honours degree.

Bolton Institute
Deane Road, Bolton BL3 5AB
Telephone: 01204 528851
Offers 'pathways' in Film and
Television Studies and Creative
Writing as part of its BA/B.Sc. (Hons.)
modular programme.

Bournemouth University
Talbot Campus, Fern Barrow, Poole,
Dorset BH12 5BB
Telephone: 01202 524111
BA (Hons.) Multi-media Journalism;
BA (Hons.) Scriptwriting for Film and
Television; BA (Hons.)
Communication and Media
Production.

University of Brighton
Mithras House, Lewes Road, Brighton
BN2 4AT
Telephone: 01273 600900
BA (Hons.) Information and Media
Studies; DipHE Information and
Media Studies; CertHE Information
and Media Studies.

**Bristol, University of the West of
England**
St Matthias Campus, Fishponds,
Bristol BS16 2JP
Telephone: 0117 9656261
BA in Cultural and Media Studies.

Brunel University College
Twickenham Campus, 300 St
Margaret's Road, Twickenham,
Middlesex TW1 1PT
Telephone: 0181 891 0121
Film and Television Studies available
as Minor option on BA/BA (Hons.)
Integrated (modular) Degree Scheme,
although there are also plans to
introduce it as a Major.

The Buckinghamshire College
(a college of Brunel University)
Queen Alexandra Road, High
Wycombe, Bucks HP11 2JZ
Telephone: 01494 522141
BA (Hons.) Film, Media and Culture.

Canterbury Christ Church College
Canterbury, Kent CT1 1QU
Telephone: 01227 782422
Offers Radio, Film and Television
Studies as part of a BA/B.Sc.
Combined Honours degree.

**University of Central England in
Birmingham**
Perry Barr, Birmingham B42 2SU
Telephone: 0121 331 5000
BA (Hons.) Media and
Communication. Postgraduate
Diploma in Broadcast Journalism
(NCTBJ).

University of Central Lancashire, Dept of Journalism
Preston PR1 2HE
Telephone: 01772 201201
BA (Hons.) Journalism (NCTBJ).
Journalism, Media Studies and Media
Technology can be combined with
another one or two subjects on the
Combined Honours course.
Postgraduate Diploma in Radio and
Television Journalism (NCTBJ);
Postgraduate Diploma in Newspaper
Journalism; Pre-entry Certificate in
Newspaper Journalism.

Central Saint Martin's College of Art and Design
(part of the London Institute)
Southampton Row, London
WC1B 4AP
Telephone: 0171 753 9090
MA Fashion Journalism.

Cheltenham & Gloucester College of Higher Education
PO Box 220, The Park, Cheltenham,
Gloucestershire GL50 2QF
Telephone: 01242 532700/532824
Media Communications available as
part of a modular BA or B.Sc. degree.

Chichester Institute of Higher Education
(a college of the University of
Southampton)
Bognor Regis Campus, Upper Bognor
Road, Bognor Regis, West Sussex
PO21 1HR
Telephone: 01243 865581
Offers Media Studies as a Joint or
Minor subject on a BA (Hons.)
Combined degree.

City of Liverpool Community College
Myrtle Street, Liverpool L7 7DN
Telephone: 0151 252 1515
Access to the Media.

City University
Department of Journalism,
Northampton Square, London
EC1V OHB
Telephone: 0171 477 8221
BA in Journalism and a Social Science
(Economics, Sociology, Psychology or
Philosophy); Postgraduate Diplomas
in: Newspaper Journalism; Broadcast
Journalism; Periodical Journalism.
International Journalism Diploma or
MA.

Cornwall College
Centre for Arts, Media and Social
Sciences, Pool, Redruth, Cornwall
TR15 3RD
Telephone: 01209 712911
HNC Writing for the Media; National
Diploma in Media; NCTJ
Postgraduate Diploma.

Cumbria College of Art and Design
Brampton Road, Carlisle, Cumbria
CA3 9AY
Telephone: 01228 25333
BA (Hons.) Media.

Darlington College of Technology
(a member of the University of Teesside
partnership)
Cleveland Avenue, Darlington, County
Durham DL3 7BB
Telephone: 01325 503050
Pre-entry course for Newspaper
Journalism; Postgraduate Diploma in
Radio Journalism; International

Diploma course in Journalism. Also block release and refresher courses. BA (Hons.) Journalism.

Dartington College of Arts
Totnes, Devon TQ9 6EJ
Telephone: 01803 863234/862224
Single Honours degree in Performance Writing; also offered as a Major or Minor subject on a Combined Honours degree.

De Montfort University
The Gateway, Leicester LE1 9BH
Telephone: 0116 2551551
Offers Media Studies as a Single Honours subject or as part of a Joint or Combined Honours degree.
Postgraduate Diploma in Journalism.

University of Derby
Kedleston Road, Derby DE22 1GB
Telephone: 01332 622222
BA (Hons.) Film and Television Studies; also available as a Minor, Joint or Major option on a Combined modular course, leading to a CertHE, a DipHE or a degree. MA Degree in Film and Television Studies; also available as a Postgraduate Certificate or Diploma.

Dundee College of Further Education
Constitution Road Centre, Dundee DD3 6TB
Telephone: 01382 834834
HNC in Radio Broadcasting.

University of East Anglia
Norwich, NR4 7TJ
Telephone: 01603 456161
BA Media Studies with Honours Language.

University of East London
Barking Campus, Longbridge Road, Dagenham, Essex RM8 2AS
Telephone: 0181 590 7722
BA (Hons.) Media Studies; also available as a Major, Minor or Joint option on a Combined degree.

East Surrey College
Media Division, Gatton Point North, Claremont Road, Redhill, Surrey RH1 2JX
Telephone: 01737 772611
Foundation in Journalism.

Falmouth College of Arts
Woodlane, Falmouth, Cornwall TR11 4RA
Telephone: 01326 211077
BA (Hons.) Broadcasting Studies; BA (Hons.) Journalism Studies; Postgraduate Diploma in Broadcast Journalism (NCTBJ).

University of Glamorgan
Prifysgol Morgannwg, Pontypridd, Mid Glamorgan CF37 1DL
Telephone: 01443 480480
Media Studies available as part of Joint or Major/Minor Honours degrees, or on the Combined Studies programme.
BA (Hons.) Communication Studies.

Glasgow Caledonian University
City Campus, Cowcaddens Road, Glasgow G4 0BA
Telephone: 0141 331 3000
BA/BA (Hons.) Communication and Mass Media.
See also Scottish Centre for Journalism Studies.

Gloucestershire College of Arts & Technology
Brunswick Campus, Brunswick Road, Gloucester GL1 1HU
Telephone: 01452 426549
Professional pre-entry course for Newspaper Journalism (NCTJ).

Goldsmiths College
University of London, New Cross, London SE14 6NW
Telephone: 0171 919 7171
BA (Hons.) in Communications; MAs in: Journalism; Radio; Television Documentary; Television Drama.

University of Greenwich
Wellington Street, Woolwich, London SE18 6PF
Telephone: 0181 316 8590/331 8000
BA/BA (Hons.) Media and Communication.

Gwent College of Higher Education
PO Box 101, Newport, Gwent NP6 1YH
Telephone: 01633 432432
BA (Hons.) Cultural and Media Studies.

Gwent Tertiary College
Pontypool and Usk Campus, Blaendare Road, Pontypool, Gwent NP4 5YE
Telephone: 01495 755141
Professional pre-entry course for Newspaper Journalism (NCTJ).

Harlow College
West Site, The High, Harlow, Essex CM20 1LT
Telephone: 01279 868000
Block release courses; postgraduate course; pre-entry course; HND.

Highbury College
Faculty of Media & Community Education, Dovercourt Road, Cosham, Portsmouth, Hants PO6 2SA
Telephone: 01705 383131
Pre-entry course in Newspaper Journalism (NCTJ); pre-entry course in Magazine Journalism; Postgraduate Diploma in Broadcast Journalism (NCTBJ); Access to Journalism and Media Studies. Also runs block release courses.

University of Humberside
Cottingham Road, Hull HU6 7RT
Telephone: 01482 440550
BA (Hons.) Media; BA (Hons.) European Media; HND Media Production.

King Alfred's College
Winchester, Hampshire SO22 4NR
Telephone: 01962 841515
Media, Film and Communication is an option on the BA/B.Sc. (Hons.) Combined Studies.

Lambeth College
Vauxhall Centre, Belmore Street, Wandsworth Road, London SW8 2JY
Telephone: 0171 501 5424
Access to Journalism; Pre-entry Certificate in Newspaper Journalism (both for members of Black and Asian communities only).

University of Leeds
Leeds LS2 9JT
Telephone: 0113 2333999
BA in Broadcasting Studies/Bachelor of Broadcasting (in co-operation with BBC Television Training); BA (Hons.) Communications.

Leeds, Trinity and All Saints
Brownberrie Lane, Horsforth, Leeds
LS18 5HD
Telephone: 0113 2837123
Offers Media as half of a Joint BA
(Hons.).

Liverpool John Moores University
58 Hope Street, Liverpool L1 9EB
Telephone: 0151 231 2000/5006
BA (Hons.) Media and Cultural
Studies; BA (Hons.) Media
Professional Studies; Journalism
Studies and Media and Cultural
Studies are offered as part of a Joint
degree.

London College of Fashion
(part of the London Institute)
20 John Princes Street, London
W1M 0BJ
Telephone: 0171 514 7400
BA (Hons.) Fashion Promotion
(includes study of radio, TV and print
journalism); Access to Fashion
Promotion Media course (modules
include writing skills, general
journalism, fashion journalism and
multimedia).

**London College of Printing and
Distributive Trades**
(part of the London Institute)
Elephant and Castle, London SE1 6SB
Telephone: 0171 514 6500
Postgraduate Diplomas in: Radio
Journalism; European Journalism;
Photojournalism; Printing and
Publishing Studies. Graduate Diploma
in Periodical Journalism; BA (Hons.)
Journalism; BA (Hons.) Media Studies;
BA (Hons.) Publishing; Foundation
Course in Media Studies; BTEC
HND in Journalism. Also runs a

number of short professional courses
in media, for example, English for
Journalists, Writing for Magazines,
Sub-editing, Layout for Journalists.

London Institute *See Central Saint
Martin's College of Art and Design, London
College of Fashion and London College of
Printing and Distributive Trades.*

**Loughborough University of
Technology**
Loughborough, Leicestershire
LE11 3TU Telephone: 01509 263171
BA (Hons.) Information and
Publishing Studies; B.Sc. (Hons.)
Communication and Media Studies.

University of Luton
Park Square, Luton, Beds LU1 3JU
Telephone: 01582 34111
BA (Hons.) Media Practices; BA
(Hons.) Media Production; Media
Practices, Media Performance, Media
Production, Media Technology and
Journalism are also available as options
on a Combined degree.

**Manchester Metropolitan
University**
Department of Communication
Media, Chatham Building, Cavendish
Street, All Saints, Manchester M15 6BR
Telephone: 0161 247 1284/2000
BA (Hons.) Interactive and Broadcast
Media. Writing is an option on both
BA (Hons.) Creative Arts and BA
(Hons.) Humanities courses.

Middlesex University
Trent Park, Bramley Road, London
N14 4XS
Telephone: 0181 362 5000
BA (Hons.) Media & Cultural Studies;
also available as a Major, combined

with one or two other subjects. BA
(Hons.) Writing; BA (Hons.) Writing &
Publishing Studies available as a Major
combined with one or two other
subjects; HND Journalism (run jointly
with Harlow College).

Napier University
219 Colinton Road, Edinburgh
EH14 1DJ
Telephone: 0131 444 2266
BA Journalism Studies; BA
Publishing; block release courses.

Nene College
Park Campus, Boughton Green Road,
Northampton NN2 7AL
Telephone: 01604 735500
Media and Popular Culture is available
as part of a BA or B.Sc. (Hons.)
Combined Studies degree.

**The Norwich School of Art and
Design**
St George Street, Norwich, Norfolk
NR3 1BB
Telephone: 01603 610561
BA (Hons.) Cultural Studies has
options in Creative Writing (Media).

**North East Wales Institute of
Higher Education**
Plas Coch, Mold Road, Wrexham,
Clwyd LL11 2AW
Telephone: 01978 290666
Media Studies available as half of a
BA (Joint Hons.)

Northern Media School
School of Cultural Studies, Sheffield
Hallam University, The Workstation,
15 Paternoster Row, Sheffield S1 2BX
Telephone: 0114 2796511/2753511
Postgraduate Diploma in Broadcast
Journalism.

Nottingham Trent University
Burton Street, Nottingham NG1 4BU
Telephone: 0115 9418418
BA (Hons.) Broadcast Journalism; BA
(Hons.) Communication Studies.
Media and Cultural Studies is available
as an option on the BA (Hons.)
Humanities and BA (Hons.) Modern
European Studies degree courses.

Oxford Brookes University
Gipsy Lane Campus, Headington,
Oxford OX3 0BP
Telephone: 01865 741111
Publishing is available as part of a Joint
Honours degree. Postgraduate
Diploma in Advanced Studies in
Publishing.

University of Portsmouth
Eldon Building, Winston Churchill
Avenue, Portsmouth PO1 2DJ
Telephone: 01705 876543
BA (Hons.) Art, Design and Media.

Queen Margaret College
Clerwood Terrace, Edinburgh
EH12 8TS
Telephone: 0131 317 3000/3247
BA (Hons.) Communication Studies
(includes Media Studies); Media &
Cultural Studies is also a Major, Joint
or Minor option on the BA (Hons.) or
B.Sc. (Hons.) Combined Studies.
Subject to approval, the college will
also be offering an MA in Media and
Modern Culture.

The Robert Gordon University
Schoolhill, Aberdeen AB9 1FR
Telephone: 01224 262000
BA/BA (Hons.) Publishing Studies;
Postgraduate Certificate/Diploma/
Masters in Publishing Studies
(distance learning).

College of St Mark & St John

Derriford Road, Plymouth PL6 8BH
Telephone: 01752 777188
BA (Hons.) Media Studies.

University of Salford

Salford M5 4WT
Telephone: 0161 745 5000
BA (Hons.) Media, Language and
Business; BA (Hons.) Television and
Radio.

Scottish Centre for Journalism Studies

(run jointly by the University of
Strathclyde and Glasgow Caledonian
University)
University of Strathclyde, 26
Richmond Street, Glasgow G1 1XH
Telephone: 0141 553 4166
Postgraduate Diploma in Journalism
Studies (NCTJ); M.Litt. in Journalism
Studies; M.Litt. in Journalism
Research.

University of Sheffield

Western Bank, Sheffield S10 2TN
Telephone: 0114 2768555
BA (Hons.) Journalism Studies.

Sheffield College

Stradbroke Centre, Spinkhill Drive,
Sheffield S13 8FD
Telephone: 0114 2602700/2
Access to Journalism course;
Certificate in Foundation Journalism;
pre-entry Reporting course (NCTJ).
New 'fast-track' courses (eighteen
weeks) for graduates were introduced
in September 1995. Pre-entry
Photojournalism course (NCTJ). Also
block release courses for direct entry
trainees whose employers are putting
them through the NCTJ scheme.

Sheffield Hallam University

City Campus, Pond Street, Sheffield
S1 1WB Telephone: 0114 2720911
BA (Hons.) Media Studies.
See also Northern Media School.

Southampton Institute

East Park Terrace, Southampton,
Hampshire SO14 0YN
Telephone: 01703 319000
BA (Hons.) Journalism; BA (Hons.)
Media with Cultural Studies.

South Bank University

103 Borough Road, London SE1 0AA
Telephone: 0171 928 8989
B.Sc. (Hons.) Media and Society.

Staffordshire University

College Road, Stoke-on-Trent ST4 2DE
Telephone: 01782 294000
BA (Hons.) Film, Television and Radio
Studies; B.Eng. (Hons.) Media and
Consumer Technology.

Stevenson College

Bankheed Avenue, Sighthill,
Edinburgh EH11 4DE
Telephone: 0131 535 4600
HND in Production Skills.

University of Stirling

Stirling FK9 4LA
Telephone: 01786 473171
BA/BA (Hons.) Film & Media
Studies; M.Litt. and Ph.D. in Media
Studies.

University of Strathclyde *See Scottish
Centre for Journalism Studies.*

Suffolk College

Rope Walk, Ipswich, Suffolk IP4 1LT
Telephone: 01473 255885
BA (Hons.) Cultural and Critical
Studies (Media Studies).

University of Sunderland
Langham Tower, Ryhope Road,
Sunderland SR2 7EE
Telephone: 0191 515 3000
BA (Hons.) Media Studies; Media
Studies also available as part of a
BA/B.Sc. (Hons.) Combined
Programmes Scheme. BA (Hons.)
Communication Studies.

Surrey Institute of Art and Design
Falkner Road, Farnham, Surrey
GU9 7DS
Telephone: 01252 732286
BA (Hons.) Media Studies; BA (Hons.)
Journalism; BTEC HND Journalism.

University of Sussex
Falmer, Brighton BN1 9QN
Telephone: 01273 678416
BA (Hons.) Media Studies; MA in
Media Studies.

Trinity & All Saints
(a college of the University of Leeds)
Brownberrie Lane, Horsforth, Leeds
LS18 5HD
Telephone: 0113 2837100
BA (Hons.) Media with another
subject.

University of Ulster
Cromore Road, Coleraine, County
Derry BT52 1SA
Telephone: 01265 44141
BA (Hons.) Media Studies; Media
Studies is also available as a Major,
Joint or Minor subject on a BA (Hons.)
Humanities Combined. Postgraduate
Diploma in Media Studies; can be
followed by MA Media Studies.

University of Wales Cardiff
Centre for Journalism Studies, 69 Park
Place, Cardiff CF1 3AS

Telephone: 01222 874000/874786
Post-graduate Diploma in Journalism
Studies, with newspaper, broadcast,
magazine, public and media relations,
and photo-journalism options. MA in
Journalism Studies. Euro-MA (MA in
European Journalism Studies, with a
term each in Utrecht (The
Netherlands), Århus (Denmark) and
Cardiff. BA in Journalism, Film and
Broadcasting. M.Phil. and Ph.D. in
Journalism Studies.

University College Warrington
Padgate Campus, Fearnhead Lane,
Warrington, Cheshire WA2 0DB
Telephone: 01925 814343
Media Studies available as part of a
BA Joint Honours or Combined
Studies; MA and Postgraduate
Diplomas in: Media and Cultural
Studies; Radio and Sound Production.

West Herts College (Associate College
of the University of Hertfordshire)
Watford Campus, Hempstead Road,
Watford, Herts WD1 3EZ
Telephone: 01923 257500
B.Sc. (Hons.) Graphic Media Studies
(includes options of Media Studies and
Publishing); Postgraduate Diploma in
Writing and Production for the Media;
Postgraduate Diploma in Publishing.

University of the West of England
Faculty of Art, Media & Design,
Kennel Lodge Road, Bristol BS3 2JR
Telephone: 0117 9660222
BA (Hons.) Time-Based Media
(concentrates on programme
production in TV, radio and
multimedia).

University of Westminster
309 Regent Street, London WIR 8AL
Telephone: 0171 911 5000
BA (Hons.) Media Studies; MA in
Journalism Studies; Postgraduate
Diploma in Journalism. Short courses
in media studies and desktop
publishing.

University of Wolverhampton
Wolverhampton WV1 1SB
Telephone: 01902 321000
BA (Hons.) Media and
Communication Studies; Media &
Communication Studies available as
Major, Joint or Minor option on BA
(Hons.) modular degree scheme.

Wulfrun College
Paget Road, Wolverhampton WV6 0DU
Telephone: 01902 317700
Runs a variety of media courses,
including NCTJ day-release course,
BTEC National Diploma, and
evening courses in journalism and
radio skills.

Yale College
Wrexham FE Centre, Grove Park
Road, Wrexham, Clwyd LL12 7AA
Telephone: 01978 311794
Day-release courses for NCTJ
trainees.

Vocational Training Courses

Some of these courses are open to all; others are intended for
people already working in the industry but will often allow the odd
'outsider' in as well so it's always worth asking (and that way you
start making contacts within the industry as well as training).
Prices and course content vary hugely so shop around before you
buy.

Book House Training Centre
45 East Hill, Wandsworth, London
SW18 2QZ
Telephone: 0181 874 2718/4608
Offers short, daytime courses in
proofreading, copy editing and picture
research aimed at people already
working in the industry but will
sometimes take outsiders. Recently
started distance-learning courses in
proofreading and copy editing.

Central Office of Information
(Film section) Room 731, Hercules
Road, London SE1 7DU
Telephone: 0171 261 8652
Courses in news and feature writing.

Chapterhouse Publishing
2 Southernhay West, Exeter EX1 1JG
Telephone: 01392 499488
Residential and correspondence
courses in proofreading and copy
editing.

Communications Skills Europe Ltd
Paramount House, 104–108 Oxford
Street, London W1N 9FA
Telephone: 0171 580 6312
Range of one- and two-day courses
on subjects such as news and feature
writing, subbing and reporting.

Community Radio Association
15 Paternoster Row, Sheffield S1 2BX
Telephone: 0114 2795219
Runs a small number of three-month
radio production courses.

**Cotswold and Swindon News
Service**
101 Bath Road, Swindon, Wiltshire
SN1 4AX
Telephone: 01793 485461
Courses cover basic journalism
techniques, including interviewing and
note-taking, feature research and
development, and legal aspects.

CSV Media
237 Pentonville Road, St Pancras,
London N1 9NJ
Telephone: 0171 278 6601
Produces broadcast programmes for
and about volunteer groups. Runs
evening courses in London on radio
reporting and production.

EMAP Training
4th Floor, 57 Priestgate, Peterborough
PE1 1JW
Telephone: 01733 892444/0171 436
1515
Mainly dedicated to providing training
for EMAP staff, but there are also
external places available on its twice-
yearly, twenty-week newspaper and
magazine journalism course, including
law, government, shorthand and
keyboard skills.

Journalism Training Centre
Unit G, Mill Green Business Park, Mill
Green Road, Mitcham, Surrey
CR4 4HT
Telephone: 0181 640 3696
Runs a fifteen-week NVQ Core Skills
Certificate course, covering subjects
including news reporting, shorthand,
feature writing, sub-editing,
interviewing techniques, proofreading
and word processing.

London School of Publishing
86 Old Brompton Road, London
SW7 3LQ
Telephone: 0171 221 3399
Runs evening courses in many aspects
of publishing.

Magnus Carter Associates
13 Dowry Square, Bristol BS8 4SL
Telephone: 0117 9244028
Runs a number of media courses for
individuals or businesses.

NCTJ
Short Course Department, Latton
Bush Centre, Southern Way, Harlow,
Essex CM18 7BL
Telephone: 01279 430009
Runs a variety of courses, lasting from
one to five days, on subjects from
sharpening your English to
introduction to QuarkXPress.

**National Film and Television
School**
Beaconsfield Studios, Station Road,
Beaconsfield, Bucks HP9 1LG
Telephone: 01494 671234/677903
Three-year full-time courses in writing,
directing and producing. The National
Short Course Training Programme, a
separate unit within the School,

provides short practical courses in all aspects of working in film and TV, from directing to scriptwriting, to presenting and interviewing techniques. The vast majority are technical and most are aimed at people who've been in the industry for at least two years, but there are also foundation courses for beginners.

PMA Training
Administrative Offices: The Old Anchor, Church Street, Hemingford Grey, Cambs PE18 9DF
Telephone: 01480 300653
Runs a wide variety of short courses, on everything from learning to write, sub and commission, to how to be a deputy editor, to surviving as a freelance. All courses take place in London.

Radio Worldwide Training Unit
Springhead Park House, Park Lane, Rothwell, Leeds LS26 0EP
Telephone: 0113 2822291
Runs two-week beginners' courses.

Television and Radio Training Unit
Derwent Business Centre, Clarke Street, Derby DE1 2BU
Telephone: 01332 296684
Runs a variety of courses throughout the country, from Production Researcher's Workshop to Compiling a Bulletin to Basic Journalism Skills. Prices start at just under £120 for a one-day course.

Vera Productions
30–38 Dock Street, Leeds LS10 1JF
Telephone: 0113 2428646
All-women video company that also runs short video production training courses for other women in and around Leeds.

WAVES (Women's Audio Visual Education Scheme)
The Wheel, 4 Wild Court, London WC2B 4AU
Telephone: 0171 430 1076
Runs broadcast-related training courses for women, some specifically for women who have been registered unemployed for at least six months, often free.

Society of Freelance Editors and Proofreaders
Runs a variety of courses in London (and sometimes York and Edinburgh) covering all aspects of the industry, from an introduction to proofreading to brushing up grammar to going freelance.

Open and Distance Learning Courses

Bear in mind that correspondence courses (other than the NCTJ's own distance-learning package) are not formally recognized or recommended by people in the industry and they certainly can't guarantee you work at the end. However, if you're starting completely from scratch or can't attend a training centre, you may find them helpful – and they do show that you're keen.

The London School of Journalism
PO Box 1745, Bath BA2 6YE
Telephone: 01225 444774
Offers a number of open learning
courses in journalism; start any time
you like and take up to two years to
complete. Also runs short tutorial
courses (full-time, day release and
evening) and a full-time six-month
tutorial course in General Journalism.

Cheltenham Tutorial College
292 High Street, Cheltenham, Glos
GL50 3HQ
Telephone: 01242 241279
Has a course in freelance journalism,
as well as courses in shorthand (three
kinds) and keyboard skills.

National Extension College
18 Brooklands Avenue, Cambridge
CB2 2HN
Telephone: 01223 316644
Correspondence course in copy
editing.

**National Council for the Training of
Journalists**
Latton Bush Centre, Southern Way,
Harlow, Essex CM18 7BL
Telephone: 01279 430009

Has distance-learning courses in
newspaper journalism, periodical
journalism, sub-editing, and media law
for periodical journalists.

The Open Learning Centre
24 King Street, Carmarthen, Dyfed
SA31 1BS
Telephone: 01267 235268
Offers several journalism courses,
including 'Writing for the Periodical
Press', 'Freelance and Feature Writing',
'Sub-editing' and 'Journalism and
Newswriting'.

The Writers Bureau
Sevendale House, 7 Dale Street,
Manchester M1 1JB
Telephone: 0161 228 2362
Has a creative writing course, which
includes modules on fiction writing as
well as different kinds of journalism.
There is no time limit on completing
the course.

Check also under Professional
Associations and Networks for other
organizations offering training to
members.

Chapter 10 / **Useful Addresses (1)**
Professional and
Trade Associations

Association of Independent Radio Companies (AIRC)
Radio House, 46 Westbourne Grove, London W2 5SH
Telephone: 0171 727 2646
The trade association for independent radio companies in the UK, it provides a careers information leaflet and details of radio training courses. Owns the Network Chart Show.

BARB (Broadcasters Audience Research Board Ltd)
Glenthorne House, Hammersmith Grove, London W6 OND
Telephone: 0181 741 9110

BBC Recruitment Services
PO Box 7000, London W5 2WY
Telephone: 0181 749 7000
Can supply a booklet, *The Way In*, listing BBC jobs in radio and television.

Book House Training Centre
45 East Hill, Wandsworth, London SW18 2QZ
Telephone: 0181 874 2718/4608
Can send you a copy of *Careers in Book Publishing*, a leaflet produced by the Publishers Association, plus details of

universities and colleges offering diploma and degree courses in publishing. It has a mail-order operation, Book Publishing Books, which specializes in titles specific to the industry; they can send a catalogue.

Book Trust
Book House, 45 East Hill, Wandsworth, London SW18 2QZ
Telephone: 0181 870 9055
An independent charity working to promote books and authors. Administers literary prizes, including the Booker. The Information Service can answer queries about books and reading. Also has an office in Scotland (see below).

Book Trust Scotland
The Scottish Book Centre, 137 Dundee Street, Edinburgh EH11 1BG
Telephone: 0131 229 3663

British Association of Journalists
88 Fleet Street, London EC4Y 1PJ
Telephone: 0171 353 3003
Acts as a trade union for journalists working in all branches of the media.

British Film Institute (BFI)
21 Stephen Street, London W1P 1PL
Telephone: 0171 255 1444
Produces a large number of media
publications, including *Media Courses
UK* (annual, edited by Lavinia Orton;
a comprehensive guide to media-
related courses nation-wide). Good
library facilities.

**British Kinematograph Sound and
Television Society (BKSTS)**
M6–14 Victoria House, Vernon Place,
London WC1B 4DJ
Telephone: 0171 242 8400
Union for people employed in the
technical areas of film, television,
sound or related industries. Students
on relevant training courses can join
for £15.

**Broadcasting Complaints
Commission**
5–8 The Sanctuary, London SW1P 3JS
Telephone: 0171 233 0544
Independent statutory body which
adjudicates upon complaints of unjust
or unfair treatment or unwarranted
infringement of privacy in radio and
television programmes. Shares
premises with the Broadcasting
Standards Council (as from early
1996) and will eventually merge with
them.

**Broadcasting Entertainment
Cinematograph & Theatre Union
(BECTU)**
111 Wardour Street, London W1V 4AY
Telephone: 0171 437 8506
Union for people working in film,
broadcast and theatre. Students on
media courses can become associate
members for £10 a year. The union will

chase companies who fail to pay
freelance members.

Broadcasting Standards Council
5–8 The Sanctuary, London SW1P 3JS
Telephone: 0171 233 0544
Consider complaints about violence,
sexual conduct, taste and decency in
both programmes and ads.

**The Cable Communications
Association**
The Fifth Floor, Artillery House,
Artillery Row, London SW1P 1RT
Telephone: 0171 222 2900
The trade association for cable
companies. Can provide general
information on the cable industry and
tell you the name of the cable
franchisor for your area.

**The Chartered Institute of
Journalists**
2 Dock Offices, Surrey Quays Road,
London SE16 2XL
Telephone: 0171 252 1187
Acts as a professional body
encouraging high standards and as a
non-affiliated trade union protecting
members' interests. Has around 2,000
members working in all branches of
the media. Produces a leaflet, *What a
Journalist Does*, and can send a copy of
the NCTJ leaflet *A World of Challenge*.

**Commonwealth Broadcasting
Association**
Room 312, BBC Yalding House,
152–156 Great Portland Street, London
W1N 6AJ
Telephone: 0171 765 5144
An association of broadcasting
organizations in Commonwealth
countries. Its annual book, *Who's Who*

in Commonwealth Broadcasting contains details of English-speaking TV and radio stations (£10 to non-members).

Community Radio Association
15 Paternoster Row, Sheffield S1 2BX
Telephone: 0114 2795219
UK membership body for community radio stations. Provides information, advice and training to existing stations and to those wanting to set one up. Runs a mail-order publications service. Publishes a quarterly newsletter, *Airflash*. Has an information leaflet on RSLs (Restricted Service Licences).

Hospital Broadcasting Association
Central Office, PO Box 2481, London W2 1JR
Telephone: 0171 402 8815
Registered charity; membership body of independent hospital broadcasting stations. Provides help and support to members plus engineering services, and some specialist pre-recorded programmes. Publishes its own magazine, *On Air* (£2).

ITV Network Centre
200 Gray's Inn Road, London WC1X 8HF
Telephone: 0171 843 8000
The Careers Information Service can provide information on working in ITV.

Independent Television Commission (ITC)
33 Foley Street, London W1P 7LB
Telephone: 0171 255 3000
Administrative body, responsible for licensing and regulating all commercially funded television services provided in and from the UK,

including ITV, Channel 4, the new Channel 5, public teletext and a range of cable and satellite services (but excluding the BBC and S4C). It does this through codes on programme content, advertising sponsorship and technical standards. Does not employ programme-making staff. Publishes an annual Factfile containing information on the ITC and contacts for all the TV stations, cable system operators and other industry organizations. It also has a variety of information leaflets and a quarterly magazine, *Spectrum*, with comment and debate on television policy and practice. For details, contact the Information Office who can also give you the address of your regional ITC office.

Joint Advisory Committee for the Training of Radio Journalists c/o NUJ (address below; NUJ will forward correspondence).
Publishes a leaflet, *Careers for Journalists in Local Radio*.

National Association of Press Agencies
41 Lansdowne Crescent, Leamington Spa, Warwickshire CV32 4PR
Telephone: 01926 424181
Has a handbook listing members' names, addresses and main services provided.

The National Council for the Training of Broadcast Journalists (NCTBJ)
188 Lichfield Court, Sheen Road, Richmond, Surrey TW9 1BB
Telephone: 0181 940 0694
Voluntary body composed of representatives from the radio and

television industry, the NUJ and colleges offering courses in broadcast journalism. Works to ensure industry standards of training are maintained and grants recognition to courses which meet their requirements. Will send a leaflet, *A Future in Broadcast Journalism?*

National Council for the Training of Journalists (NCTJ)

Latton Bush Centre, Southern Way, Harlow, Essex CMI8 7BL
Telephone: 01279 430009
Publishes a booklet, *A World of Challenge*. Issues its own National Certificate to suitably qualified journalists, accredits colleges and training courses, delivers NVQs. Also runs short courses for practising journalists, on, for example, feature writing, layout and design skills, subbing, interviewing, QuarkXPress, etc. Also runs four distance learning courses leading to NVQs.

National Union of Journalists (NUJ)

Acorn House, 314–320 Gray's Inn Road, London WCIX 8DP
Telephone: 0171 278 7916
The best-known of the journalists' unions, with around 30,000 members working in newspapers, magazines, broadcasting and book publishing. The NUJ publishes a free leaflet, *Careers in Journalism*. Can supply a list of NUJ-approved journalism courses (at access, open pre-entry and postgraduate levels) run at various centres around the country. NUJ approval of a course enables its students to become temporary members of the Union free of charge, and to obtain a press card.

The Newspaper Society

Bloomsbury House, Bloomsbury Sq, 74–77 Great Russell Street, London WCIB 3DA
Telephone: 0171 636 7014
Publishes a brief leaflet, *Training to be a Journalist*, for people wanting to break into newspaper journalism.

PACT (The Producers Alliance for Cinema and Television)

Gordon House, 10 Greencoat Place, London SWIP IPH
Telephone: 0171 233 6000
Trade association for independent film and television producers. Can send a copy of the Skillset (*q.v.*) Careers Information pack.

The Periodicals Training Council (PTC)

Imperial House, 15–19 Kingsway, London WC2B 6UN
Telephone: 0171 836 8798
Training arm of the PPA (Periodical Publishers Assocation). Publishes a leaflet, *A Career in Magazines*.

PPA

See *Periodicals Training Council*, above.

Press Complaints Commission

1 Salisbury Square, London EC4Y 8AE
Telephone: 0171 353 1248
Considers complaints about invasion of privacy, dubious journalistic tactics, unfair articles, etc.

The Publishers Association

19 Bedford Square, London WCIB 3HJ
Telephone: 0171 580 6321
Can provide a leaflet, *Careers in Book Publishing.*

The Radio Academy
PO Box 4SZ, London WIA 4SZ
Telephone: 0171 323 3837
The professional body for those
working in or with an interest in radio.
Organizes seminars, conferences and
other events. Its *Yearbook* (£9.99)
contains a comprehensive directory of
radio-related contacts. Publishes a
monthly newsletter *Off Air* and mid-
year glossy magazine, *RADiO*.

The Radio Authority
Holbrook House, 14 Great Queen
Street, London WC2B 5DG
Telephone: 0171 430 2724
Awards licences to independent radio
stations (national and local, including
community, cable, satellite, student and
hospital radio and RSLs), plans
frequencies and regulates
programming and advertising. Funded
by annual fees from licensees. Can
supply a pocket book containing
names, addresses and phone numbers
of independent radio stations within
the UK and the NCTBJ leaflet *A
Future in Broadcast Journalism?* Issues
guidance notes for applications for
RSLs.

**RAJAR (RAdio Joint Audience
Research Ltd)**
Collier House, 163–169 Brompton
Road, London SW3 1PY
Telephone: 0171 584 3003
Jointly owned by the BBC and AIRC,
RAJAR carries out radio audience
surveys both national and local on a
quarterly basis.

Royal Television Society
Holborn Hall, 100 Gray's Inn Road,
London WC1X 8AL
Telephone: 0171 430 1000
Organizes courses and conferences for
and about the television industry.
Publishes a careers leaflet, *I Want to
Work in Television*. Has members in all
areas of the broadcasting industry.
Head office is in London, but there are
also regional offices which organize
events.

**Satellite and Cable Broadcasters
Group**
34 Grand Avenue, London N10 3BP
Telephone: 0181 444 4891

Scottish Daily Newspaper Society
Merchants House Buildings, 30
George Square, Glasgow G2 1EG
Telephone: 0141 248 2375

Scottish Publishers Association
137 Dundee Street, Edinburgh
EH11 1BG
Telephone: 0131 228 6866
Aimed at those who have already
published books but also organizes
training courses in aspects of
publishing and seminars on industry
issues which are open to non-members.
Publishes an annual *Directory of
Publishing in Scotland*, which includes
information on Scottish publishers,
booksellers, writers' groups and related
organizations.

Skillset
124 Horseferry Road, London
SW1P 2TX
Telephone: 0171 306 8585
The training organization for the
broadcast, film and video industries.
Produces a useful Careers Information
Pack.

Society of Freelance Editors and Proofreaders
38 Rochester Road, London NW1 9JJ
Telephone: 0171 813 3113
Aimed at those already working as freelance editors and proofreaders; inexperienced people are welcome to join but are warned that it's no guarantee of getting work. Organizes meetings and training sessions (in London, York and Edinburgh) and publishes a regular newsletter. Will provide an information pack, for which a fee is charged; call for details.

Society of Picture Researchers and Editors (SPREd)
BM Box 259, London WC1N 3XX
Telephone: 0171 405 5011/431 9886
Professional body for those already working in picture research. Produces a quarterly magazine, available to non-members.

Society of Women Writers & Journalists
110 Whitehall Road, Chingford, London E4 6DW
Telephone: 0181 529 0886

Student Radio Association
c/o Suzanne Cuff, Redwood Grore, Bredgar, Nr Sittingbourne, Kent ME9 8EP
Telephone: 01622 884418

Networks

Networking
Vera Productions, 30–38 Dock Street, Leeds LS10 1JF
Telephone: 0113 242 8646
Membership organization for women involved or interested in film, video and TV. Members receive a quarterly newsletter, inclusion in their contacts index, advice and information service.

Reel Women
57 Holmewood Gardens, London SW2 3NB
Telephone: 0181 678 7404
Network for women in film, video and television. Organizes seminars, workshops, social events.

Women in Cable UK
PO Box 4812, London SW1P 1XP
Telephone: 0171 222 2900
For women at all levels of the cable and satellite industry. Acts as a network and runs conferences, seminars, training workshops and social events for members.

Women in Film and Television
Garden Studios, 11–15 Betterton Street, London WC2H 9BP
Telephone: 0171 379 0344
Activities include workshops, seminars, networking evenings and annual awards. Open to women with a minimum of three years' professional experience in the film and television industry.

Women in Journalism

10 Oak House, Trinity Road, London
N22 4YT
Telephone: 0181 889 7526/0181 566
2908
Network set up in 1995 to represent
women in newspapers and magazines.
Conducts research on the
employment, treatment and
promotion of women journalists, and
organizes social events and seminars.
Membership is open to women with at
least two years' experience in
journalism.

Women in Publishing

c/o 12 Dyott Street, London WC1A 1DF
Telephone: 0171 916 7603
Open to all women interested in book
publishing with the aim of supporting
and encouraging them; has a
Mentoring Network and organizes
practical training courses run by senior
women in the industry (on, for
example, basic book production,
working freelance, the copy-editor's
role, the commissioning editor's role,
etc.). For details of courses, contact
Karin Horowitz, WiP Training Officer,
Gosfield House, Negus Yard,
Homerton Street, Cambridge CB2 2NZ
Telephone: 01223 414065

Women's Radio Group

90 De Beauvoir Road, London N1 4EN
Telephone: 0171 241 3729
Arts charity providing training and
networking seminars for women in all
areas of radio. Annual membership
(1995): £15 waged; £5 unwaged.

Women Writers Network

c/o Cathy Smith, Membership
Secretary, 23 Prospect Road, London
NW2 2JU
Telephone: 0171 794 5861
Network open to working women
writers and editors, freelance or staff.
Members get a monthly newsletter,
free monthly meetings with expert
speakers, discounts on WWN
seminars and workshops, and a
membership directory. Also has
regional branches in Derbyshire and
North Yorkshire.

The Writers' Guild of Great Britain

430 Edgware Road, London W2 1EH
Telephone: 0171 723 8074
A TUC-affiliated trade union
lobbying and campaigning for the
interests of writers working in books,
film, radio, multimedia, television and
theatre. Issues a regular newsletter,
organizes workshops and seminars,
provides advice on contracts, agents,
legal protection, etc.

Chapter 11 / **Useful Addresses (2) Newspaper and Magazine Companies**

Newspapers

National dailies

Daily Express
Express Newspapers plc, Ludgate House, 245 Blackfriars Road, London SE1 9UX
Telephone: 0171 928 8000

Daily Mail
Associated Newspapers Ltd, Northcliffe House, 2 Derry Street, London W8 5TT
Telephone: 0171 938 6000

Daily Mirror
MGN Ltd, 1 Canada Square, Canary Wharf, London E14 5AP
Telephone: 0171 293 3000

Daily Record (in Scotland)
40 Anderston Quay, Glasgow G3 8DA
Telephone: 0141 248 7000

Daily Sport
Sport Newspapers Ltd, 19 Great Ancoats Street, Manchester M60 4BT
Telephone: 0161 236 4466

Daily Star
As for *Daily Express*
Telephone: 0171 928 8000

The Daily Telegraph
The Telegraph plc, 1 Canada Square, Canary Wharf, London E14 5DT
Telephone: 0171 538 5000

The European
200 Gray's Inn Road, London WC1X 8NE
Telephone: 0171 418 7777

Financial Times
1 Southwark Bridge, London SE1 9HL
Telephone: 0171 873 3000

The Guardian
Guardian Newspapers Ltd, 119 Farringdon Road, London EC1R 3ER
Telephone: 0171 278 2332

The Herald
Caledonian Newspapers Ltd, 195 Albion Street, Glasgow G1 1QP
Telephone: 0141 552 6255

Independent
Newspaper Publishing plc, 1 Canada Square, Canary Wharf, London E14 5DL
Telephone: 0171 293 2000

Morning Star
The Morning Star Co-operative
Society Ltd, 1–3 Ardleigh Road,
London N1 4HS
Telephone: 0171 254 0033

The Scotsman
The Scotsman Publications Ltd, 20
North Bridge, Edinburgh EH1 1YT
Telephone: 0131 225 2468

The Sun
News Group Newspapers Ltd, 1
Virginia Street, Wapping, London
E1 9BD
Telephone: 0171 782 4000

The Times
Times Newspapers Ltd, 1 Virginia
Street, Wapping, London E1 9XN
Telephone: 0171 782 5000/7000

National Sundays

The Independent on Sunday
Newspaper Publishing plc, 1 Canada
Square, London E14 5AP
Telephone: 0171 293 2000

The Mail on Sunday
Associated Newspapers Ltd,
Northcliffe House, 2 Derry Street,
Kensington, London W8 5TT
Telephone: 0171 938 6000

News of the World
News Group Newspapers Ltd, 1
Virginia Street, Wapping, London
E1 9BD
Telephone: 0171 782 4000

The Observer
Guardian Newspapers Ltd, 119
Farringdon Road, London EC1R 3ER
Telephone: 0171 278 2332

The People
MGN Ltd, 1 Canada Square,
Canary Wharf, London E14 5AP
Telephone: 0171 510 3000

Scotland on Sunday
The Scotsman Publications Ltd, 20
North Bridge, Edinburgh EH1 1YT
Telephone: 0131 225 2468

Sunday Express
Express Newspapers plc, Ludgate
House, 245 Blackfriars Road, London
SE1 9UX
Telephone: 0171 928 8000

Sunday Mirror
MGN Ltd, 1 Canada Square,
Canary Wharf, London E14 1AB
Telephone: 0171 510 3000

Sunday Post
DC Thomson & Co Ltd, 2 Albert
Square, Dundee DD1 9QJ
Telephone: 01382 223131

Sunday Sport
Sport Newspapers Ltd, 19 Great
Ancoats Street, Manchester M60 4BT
Telephone: 0161 236 4466

The Sunday Telegraph
The Telegraph plc, 1 Canada Square,
Canary Wharf, London E14 5DT
Telephone: 0171 538 5000

The Sunday Times
Times Newspapers Ltd, 1 Virginia
Street, London E1 9BD
Telephone: 0171 782 5000

Wales on Sunday
Western Mail & Echo Ltd, Thomson
House, Havelock Street, Cardiff
CF1 1XR
Telephone: 01222 223333

Main Regional Newspaper Groups

Most of these groups are made up of several branches in different
parts of the country; the addresses given are those of the head
office.

Argus Newspapers Ltd
Argus House, Crowhurst Road,
Hollingbury, Brighton BN1 8AR
Telephone: 01273 544544

Croydon Advertiser Group Ltd
Advertiser House, Brighton Road,
South Croydon CR2 6UB
Telephone: 0181 668 4111

Courier Newspapers
Longfield Road, North Farm
Industrial Estates, Tunbridge Wells,
Kent TN2 3HL
Telephone: 01892 540212

**Eastern Counties Newspapers
Group**
Prospect House, Rouen Road,
Norwich, Norfolk NR1 1RE
Telephone: 01603 628311

EMAP Newspapers Ltd
Roebuck House, 33 Broad Street,
Stamford, Lincs PE9 1RB
Telephone: 01780 66566
Publishes just under 100 regional
newspapers.

Guardian Media Group plc
164 Deansgate, Manchester M60 2RD
Telephone: 0161 832 7200

**Home Counties Newspapers
(Holdings) plc**
63 Campfield Road, St Albans,
Hertfordshire AL1 5HX
Telephone: 01727 866166

Johnston Press plc
53 Manor Place, Edinburgh EH3 7EG
Telephone: 0131 225 3361

**Midland Independent Newspapers
plc**
28 Colmore Circus, Queensway,
Birmingham, West Midlands B4 6AX
Telephone: 0121 236 3366

Midland News Association Ltd
51–53 Queen Street, Wolverhampton,
West Midlands WV1 3BU
Telephone: 01902 313131

Morton Newspapers Ltd
21 Windsor Avenue, Lurgan,
Craigavon, Co Armagh BT67 9BQ
Telephone: 01762 326161

Northcliffe Newspapers Group Ltd
(part of Associated Newspapers)
31 John Street, London WC1N 2QB
Telephone: 0171 400 1100

**Portsmouth & Sunderland
Newspapers plc**
Buckton House, 37 Abingdon Road,
London W8 6AH
Telephone: 0171 937 9741

Newsquest Media
Newspaper House, 34–44 London
Road, Morden, Surrey SM4 5BR
Telephone: 0181 640 8989

**Scottish & Universal Newspapers
Ltd**
1 Woodside Terrace, Glasgow G3 7UY
Telephone: 0141 353 3366

Southern Newspapers plc
45 Above Bar, Southampton,
Hampshire SO14 7AA
Telephone: 01703 634134

Tindle Newspaper Group
Newspaper House, 114–115 West
Street, Farnham, Surrey GU9 7HL
Telephone: 01252 735667

Trinity International Holdings plc
6 Heritage Court, Lower Bridge
Street, Chester, Cheshire CH1 1RD
Telephone: 01244 350555

United Newspapers plc
Ludgate House, 245 Blackfriars Road,
London SE1 9UY
Telephone: 0171 921 5000

Westminster Press Ltd (part of
Pearson plc)
126 Jermyn Street, London SW1Y 4UJ
Telephone: 0171 447 3600

Press Agencies

These are some of the better known news agencies but there are
many more; see *Benn's Media*, Volume 1 for more contacts.

The Press Association
292 Vauxhall Bridge Road, London
SW1V 1AE
Telephone: 0171 963 7000

The Associated Press Ltd
12 Norwich Street, London EC4A 1BP
Telephone: 0171 353 1515

National News Agency
30 St John's Lane, London EC1M 4BJ
Telephone: 0171 417 7707

Reuters Ltd
Head office: 85 Fleet Street, London
EC4P 4AJ
Telephone: 0171 250 1122

UK News
St George Street, Leicester LE1 9FQ
Telephone: 0116 253 0022

United Press International
2 Greenwich View Place, Millharbour,
London E14 9NN
Telephone: 0171 538 5310

Magazine Publishers

There are probably hundreds of magazine companies, some publishing just one title. These are some of the more established ones – see media guides for full list. The PPA includes a list of its members in *A Career in Magazines*.

Nexus Specialist Publications
Nexus House, Boundary Way, Hemel
Hempstead, Herts HP2 7ST
Telephone: 01442 66551
Includes a number of special interest
titles along the lines of *Radio Controlled
Model Car* and *Radio Modeller*.

Attic Futura
17 Berners Street, London W1P 3DD
Telephone: 0171 636 5115
Includes *Sugar, Inside Soaps* and *TV
Hits*.

H. Bauer Publishing Ltd
Shirley House, 25–27 Camden Road,
London NW1 9LL
Telephone: 0171 284 0909
Includes *Take a Break, Bella, TV Quick*
and *That's Life*.

BBC Magazines
Woodlands, 80 Wood Lane, London
W12 OTT
Telephone: 0181 743 5588
Includes *Radio Times* (the country's
most profitable magazine) and a
number of TV-linked titles such as
BBC Gardeners' World Magazine, Clothes
Show, and *BBC Good Food*. Also has a
growing number of children's titles,
including *Live & Kicking, Girl Talk,
Playdays* and *Noddy*.

John Brown Publishing Ltd
The Boathouse, Crabtree Lane,
Fulham, London SW6 6LU
Telephone: 0171 381 6007
Publishes *Viz* and produces
magazines for clients including
Classic FM, InterCity and Virgin
Atlantic.

Centaur Communications Ltd
St Giles House, 49–50 Poland Street,
London W1V 4AX
Telephone: 0171 494 0300
Includes a number of trade titles, such
as *LeisureWeek, Marketing Week, Money
Marketing, Creative Review* and *Televisual*.

Condé Nast Publications Ltd
Vogue House, 1 Hanover Square,
London W1R OAD
Telephone: 0171 499 9080
Upmarket glossy magazine house
whose titles include *Vogue, The World of
Interiors, Tatler, GQ, House & Garden,*

Vanity Fair. Is also beginning to develop contract magazines.

Consumers' Association
2 Marylebone Road, London NW1 4DF
Telephone: 0171 830 6000
Publishes consumer-related magazines such as *Which?* and *Check it Out!*, as well as reference books like *The Good Food Guide* and *The Which? Hotel Guide*.

Dennis Publishing Ltd
19 Bolsover Street, London W1P 7HJ
Telephone: 0171 631 1433
Includes *Maxim*, plus special interest titles such as *Game Zone*, *Computer Shopper*, *Hi-Fi Choice* and *Home Entertainment*.

EMAP plc
1 Lincoln Court, Lincoln Road, Peterborough, Cambridgeshire
PE1 2RF
Telephone: 01733 68900
The EMAP empire has numerous subsidiaries and subsidiaries of subsidiaries based at different offices in London and Peterborough. EMAP Business Communications Ltd, via the following groups and others, produces a range of business titles.
• EMAP Construct:
151 Roseberry Avenue, London
EC1R 4QX
Telephone: 0171 505 6600
Titles include *Architect's Journal*, *Construction News*, *Architectural Review* and *Civil Engineer*.
• EMAP Computing:
Greater London House, Hampstead Road, London NW1 7QZ
Telephone: 0171 388 2430
Includes *PC User* and *Which Computer*.

• EMAP Media:
33–39 Bowling Green Lane, London
EC1R 0DA
Telephone: 0171 837 1212
Titles include *Broadcast*, *Media Week* and *Press Gazette*.
• EMAP Business International:
Meed House, 21 John St, London
WC1N 2BP
Telephone: 0171 404 5513/470 6200
From *Fishing News* to *Gulf Marketing Review*.
• EMAP Fashion Ltd:
67 Clerkenwell Road, London
EC1R 5BH
Telephone: 0171 417 2800
Titles include *Drapers Record* and *British Jeweller*
• EMAP Maclaren Ltd:
Maclaren House, 19 Scarbrook Road, Croydon, Surrey CR9 1QH
Telephone: 0181 277 5000
Includes *Retail Week*, *European Plastics News* and *British Baker*.

EMAP Consumer Magazines Ltd includes the following divisions publishing a number of consumer titles:
• EMAP Apex
Apex House, Oundle Road, Peterborough PE2 9NP
Telephone: 01733 898100
Titles include *Garden Answers* and *Practical Photography*.
• EMAP Elan:
Victory House, Leicester Place, London WC2H 7BP
Telephone: 0171 437 9011
Includes *ELLE*, *Just 17*, *Looks*, *New Woman*, *More!*, *Parents*, *Slimming* and *Elle Decoration*.

- EMAP Images:
Priory Court, 30–32 Farringdon Lane,
London EC1R 3AU
Telephone: 0171 972 6700
Includes *PC Review* and *Nintendo Magazine*.
- EMAP Metro:
Mappin House, 4 Winsley Street,
London W1N 7AR
Telephone: 0171 436 1515
Men's and music titles such as *FHM*, *Kerrang!*, *Q*, *Smash Hits*.
- EMAP Nationals:
Abbots Court, 34 Farringdon Lane,
London EC1R 3AV
Telephone: 0171 216 6200
Includes *Motor Cycle News* and *Performance Car*.
- EMAP Pursuit Publishing Ltd:
Bretton Court, Bretton, Peterborough
PE3 8DZ
Telephone: 01733 264666
Titles include *Angling Times*, *Athletics Weekly*, *Today's Golfer*.

Financial Times Business Enterprises Ltd
Maple House, 149 Tottenham Court
Road, London W1P 9LL
Telephone: 0171 411 4414/896 2000
Publishes a range of business titles,
from *East European Energy Report* to
Music and Copyright to *World Policy Guide*.

Fleetway Editions Ltd
Egmont House, 25–31 Tavistock Place,
London WC1H 9SU
Telephone: 0171 344 6400
Produces a number of comics, e.g. *Bugs Bunny*, *Big Value Comic*, *2000AD* and
Buster.

Forward Publishing
5 Great Pulteney Street, London
W1R 4LD
Telephone: 0171 734 2303
Contract publisher producing
magazines for clients such as Tesco,
Silk Cut and the RAC.

Future Publishing Ltd
Beauford Court, 30 Monmouth Street,
Bath BA1 2BW
Telephone: 01225 442244
Produces a number of computing and
specialist interest titles, e.g. *Classic CD*,
.net, *PC Format*, *CD ROM Today*,
Needlecraft and *Mountain Biking*. Also has
a large site on the Internet.

GE Publishing
Elme House, 133 Long Acre, London
WC2 9AD
Telephone: 0171 836 0519
Publishers of *Inspirations*.

G & J of the UK
Portland House, Stag Place, London
SW1E 5AU
Telephone: 0171 245 8700
Only a few titles but they include big-
sellers *Best* and *Prima*.

Hammerville Magazines Ltd
Regal House, Regal Way, Watford,
Hertfordshire WD2 4YJ
Telephone: 01923 237799
Publishes a range of building-trade-
related titles.

Haymarket Group
Head Office: 12–14 Anstell Street,
London W8 5TR
Telephone: 0181 943 5000
Produces a number of trade and
consumer titles, via the following
divisions:

- Haymarket Business Publications Ltd
22 Lancaster Gate, London w2 3LY
Telephone: as above
Includes *Campaign*, *Marketing* and *PR Week*.
- Haymarket Magazines Ltd
38–42 Hampton Road, Teddington, Middlesex TW11 0JE
Telephone: as above
Includes *Autocar & Motor*, *Horticulture Week* and *Practical Caravan*.
- Haymarket Medical Ltd
30 Lancaster Gate, London w2 3LP
Telephone: as above
Includes *General Practitioner* and *MIMS*.

Hello! Ltd
Wellington House, 69/71 Upper Ground, London SE1 9PQ
Telephone: 0171 334 7404

IPC Magazines Ltd (part of Reed Elsevier plc)
King's Reach Tower, Stamford Street, London SE1 9LS
Telephone: 0171 261 5000
The largest publisher of consumer magazines in the UK, with more than 50 weekly and monthly titles. The weeklies include *TV Times*, *What's on TV*, *Woman*, *Woman's Own* and *Woman's Realm*. Among the monthlies are *Woman's Journal*, *Marie Claire*, *Loaded*, *19*, *Essentials*, *Family Circle*, *Ideal Home*, *Options*, and *Wedding and Home*. Specialist and leisure titles range from *Aeroplane Monthly* to *Melody Maker*, *Sporting Gun* to *New Scientist*.

Marshall Cavendish
119 Wardour Street, London w1v 3TD
Telephone: 0171 734 6710
Publishes a range of partwork titles.

Miller-Freeman plc (part of United Newspapers plc)
Miller-Freeman House, 30 Calderwood Street, London SE18 6QH
Telephone: 0181 855 7777
Responsible, via a number of subsidiaries, for trade publications as diverse as *Travel Trade Gazette*, *Pig Farming*, *Manufacturing Chemist* and *Tunnels & Tunnelling*. Also publishes a couple of contract titles.

National Magazine Company
National Magazine House, 72 Broadwick Street, London W1V 2BP
Telephone: 0171 439 5000
Publishes some of the most successful glossy monthlies: *Cosmopolitan*, *Company*, *SHE*, *Good Housekeeping*, *Country Living*, *ZEST*, *House Beautiful*, *Harpers & Queen*, *Esquire*.

Northern & Shell plc
The Northern & Shell Tower, City Harbour, London E14 9GL
Telephone: 0171 987 5090
Publishers of *OK!*, *Penthouse* and *Chic*.

Premier Magazines
Haymarket House, 1 Oxondon Street, London SW1Y 4EE
Telephone: 0171 925 2544
Produces a number of in-flight magazines for airlines including BA.

Reader's Digest Association Ltd
Berkeley Square House, Berkeley Square, London W1X 6AB
Telephone: 0171 629 8144
Only publishes a couple of magazines, but they include the UK's biggest seller, *Reader's Digest*.

Redwood Publishing
12–26 Lexington Street, London
WIR 4HQ
Telephone: 0171 312 2600
Contract publisher producing titles for
clients including American Express,
Sainsbury, Harvey Nichols and Marks
& Spencer.

Reed Business Publishing (part of
Reed Elsevier)
Quadrant House, The Quadrant,
Sutton, Surrey SM2 5AS
Telephone: 0181 652 3500
The largest business magazine
publisher in the UK. Includes a varied
mass of titles from *Caterer & Hotelkeeper*
to *Bankers' Almanac*, *Electrical Review* to
Poultry World.

DC Thomson & Co Ltd
2 Albert Square, Dundee, DD1 9QJ
Telephone: 01382 223131
Comics include the *Beano*, *Bunty*, *Catch*
and *Shout*. Also publishes *My Weekly*
and *People's Friend* (at 80 Kingsway
East, Dundee DD4 8SL).

VNU Business Publications
VNU House, 32–34 Broadwick Street,
London WIA 2HG
Telephone: 0171 316 9000
Publishes business and computing
periodicals such as *Accountancy Age*, *PC
Week* and *Financial Director*.

John Wiley & Sons Ltd
Baffins Lane, Chichester, West Sussex
PO19 1UD
Telephone: 01243 770351
Publishes a range of highly specialized
periodicals such as *Biological Mass
Spectrometry* and *Pesticide Science and
Systems Research*.

Chapter 12 / **Useful Addresses (3) Television and radio Companies**

Television

BBC

BBC Television
Television Centre, Wood Lane,
London W12 7RJ
Telephone: 0181 743 8000

BBC Radio
Broadcasting House, Portland Place,
London W1A 1AA
Telephone: 0171 580 4468

BBC World Service
Bush House, Strand, London
WC2B 4PH
Telephone: 0171 240 3456

BBC Monitoring
Caversham Park, Reading RG4 8TZ
Telephone: 01734 472742

BBC Midlands & East

Birmingham
BBC Pebble Mill, Pebble Mill Road,
Birmingham B5 7QQ
Telephone: 0121 414 8888

Nottingham
BBC East Midlands Broadcasting
Centre, York House, Mansfield Road,
Nottingham NG1 3JB
Telephone: 0115 9550500

Norwich
BBC East, St Catherine's Close, All
Saint's Green, Norwich, Norfolk
NR1 3ND
Telephone: 01603 619331

BBC North

Manchester
BBC North, New Broadcasting
House, Oxford Road, Manchester
M60 1SJ
Telephone: 0161 200 2020

Leeds
Broadcasting Centre, Woodhouse
Lane, Leeds, West Yorkshire LS2 9PX
Telephone: 0113 2441188

Newcastle upon Tyne
BBC TV North East, Broadcasting
Centre, Barrack Road, Newcastle
upon Tyne NE99 2NE
Telephone: 0191 232 1313

BBC Northern Ireland

Belfast
Broadcasting House, Ormeau Avenue,
Belfast BT2 8HQ
Telephone: 01232 338000

BBC Scotland

Glasgow
Broadcasting House, Queen Margaret
Drive, Glasgow G12 8DG
Telephone: 0141 339 8844

Aberdeen
Broadcasting House, Beechgrove
Terrace, Aberdeen AB9 2ZT
Telephone: 01224 625233

Dundee
Nethergate Centre, 66 Nethergate,
Dundee DD1 4ER
Telephone: 01382 202481

Edinburgh
Broadcasting House, 5 Queen Street,
Edinburgh EH2 1JF
Telephone: 0131 469 4200/225 3131

BBC South

Bristol
BBC Broadcasting House,
Whiteladies Road, Bristol, Avon
BS8 2LR
Telephone: 0117 9732211

Southampton
BBC South, Broadcasting House, 10
Havelock Road, Southampton,
Hampshire SO14 7PU
Telephone: 01703 226201

Plymouth
BBC South West, Broadcasting
House, Seymour Road, Mannamead,
Plymouth, Devon PL3 5BD
Telephone: 01752 229201

Elstree
BBC Elstree Centre, Clarendon Road,
Borehamwood, Hertfordshire WD6 1JF
Telephone: 0181 953 6100

BBC Wales

Cardiff
BBC Broadcasting House, Llandaff,
Cardiff CF5 2YQ
Telephone: 01222 572888

Bangor
Broadcasting House, Bryn Meirion,
Meirion Road, Bangor, Gwynedd
LL57 2BY
Telephone: 01248 370880

Swansea
Broadcasting House, 32 Alexandra
Road, Swansea, West Glamorgan
SA1 5DT
Telephone: 01792 654986

ITV and Channel 4 Companies

Anglia Television
Anglia House, Norwich NR1 3JG
Telephone: 01603 615151
Also has offices/news centres in
London, Cambridge, Chelmsford,
Luton, Ipswich, Northampton,
Peterborough, Milton Keynes.

Border Television
Television Centre, Carlisle CA1 3NT
Telephone: 01228 25101

Carlton Broadcasting
101 St Martin's Lane, London
WC2N 4AZ
Telephone: 0171 240 4000

Central Broadcasting
Central House, Broad Street,
Birmingham B1 2JP
Telephone: 0121 643 9898
Also has offices/news centres in
Nottingham, London, Abingdon.

Channel Television
Television Centre, St Helier, Jersey,
Channel Islands JE1 3ZD
Telephone: 01534 68999
Also has an office/news centre in
Guernsey.

GMTV
The London Television Centre, Upper
Ground, London SE1 9TT
Telephone: 0171 827 7000

Grampian Television
Queen's Cross, Aberdeen AB9 2XJ
Telephone: 01224 646464
Also has offices/news centres in
Dundee and Inverness.

Granada Television
Granada Television Centre, Quay
Street, Manchester M60 9EA
Telephone: 0161 832 7211
Also has offices/news centres in
London, Liverpool, Lancaster, Chester
and Blackburn.

HTV (Cymru) Wales
The Television Centre, Culverhouse
Cross, Cardiff CF5 6XJ
Telephone: 01222 590590

HTV West
The Television Centre, Bath Road,
Bristol BS4 3HG
Telephone: 0117 977 8366
Also has offices in London.

LWT
The London Television Centre, Upper
Ground, London SE1 9LT
Telephone: 0171 620 1620
Also has offices in Manchester.

Meridian Broadcasting
Head Office: 48 Leicester Square,
London WC2H 7LY
Telephone: 0171 925 2511
Also has production/news centres in
Newbury, Maidstone, Brighton,
Bournemouth, Basingstoke, Hastings,
Reading, Dover and Salisbury.

S4C
Parc Busnes Ty Glas,
Llanishen/Llanisien,
Cardiff/Caerdydd CF4 5DU
Telephone: 01222 741400

Scottish Television
Cowcaddens, Glasgow G2 3PR
Telephone: 0141 332 9999
Also has offices in London, Edinburgh
and Manchester.

Tyne Tees Television
The Television Centre, City Road,
Newcastle upon Tyne, NE1 2AL
Telephone: 0191 261 0181
Also has offices/news centres in
Middlesbrough and York.

Ulster Television
Havelock House, Ormeau Road,
Belfast BT7 1EB
Telephone: 01232 328122
Also has offices in London.

Westcountry Television
Western Wood Way, Langage Science
Park, Plymouth PL7 5BG
Telephone: 01752 333333

Also has offices/news centres in
Barnstaple, Exeter, Penzance,
Taunton, Torquay, Truro and
Weymouth.

Yorkshire Television
The Television Centre, Leeds LS3 1JS
Telephone: 0113 2438283
Also has offices/news centres in
London, Sheffield, Hull, Ripon,
Lincoln, Grimsby, York and
Northallerton.

Channel 4
124 Horseferry Road, London
SW1P 2TX
Telephone: 0171 396 4444

Cable and Satellite TV Companies

These are just some of the main cable and satellite services. A full
list is available from the ITC (see Chapter 10) in their Factfile
booklet.

Bravo
United Artists Programming, Twyman
House, 16 Bonny Street, London
NW1 9PG
Telephone: 0171 813 5000

BSkyB
British Sky Broadcasting Ltd,
6 Centaurs Business Park, Grant Way,
Isleworth, Middlesex TW7 5QD
Telephone: 0171 705 3000

Includes Sky Movies, Sky Movies
Gold, Sky News, Sky One, Sky Soap,
Sky Sports, Sky Sports 2, Sky Travel,
The Movie Channel.

Channel One Television Ltd
60 Charlotte Street, London W1P 2AX
Telephone: 0171 209 1234

The Children's Channel
9–13 Grape Street, London WC2H 8DR
Telephone: 0171 240 3422

CMT (Country Music Television)
United Artists Programming, Twyman
House, 16 Bonny Street, London
NW1 9PG
Telephone: 0171 813 5000

CNN (Cable News Network)
CNN House, 19–22 Rathbone Place,
London W1P 1DF
Telephone: 0171 637 6800

Discovery Channel (Europe)
United Artists Limited, Twyman
House, 16 Bonny Street, London
NW1 9PG
Telephone: 0171 482 4824

European Business News
10 Fleet Place, London EC4M 7RB
Telephone: 0171 653 9300

Eurosport-UK
55 Drury Lane, London WC2B 5SQ
Telephone: 0171 468 7777

Live TV
24th Floor, 1 Canada Square, Canary
Wharf, London E14 5DJ
Telephone: 0171 293 3900

The Movie Channel
BSkyB Ltd, 6 Centaurs Business Park,
Grant Way, Isleworth, Middlesex
TW7 5DQ
Telephone: 0171 705 3000

MTV Europe
Hawley Crescent, London NW1 8TT
Telephone: 0171 284 7777

NBC Super Channel
Melrose House, 14 Limeharbour,
London E14
Telephone: 0171 418 9418

Nickelodeon
6 Centaurs Business Park, Grant Way,
Isleworth, Middlesex TW7 5DQ
Telephone: 0171 782 3116

The Parliamentary Channel
United Artists Programming, Twyman
House, 16 Bonny Street, London
NW1 9PG
Telephone: 0171 482 4824

QVC The Shopping Channel
Marcopolo House, 346 Queenstown
Road, London SW8 4NQ
Telephone: 0171 705 5600

TNT
Turner Network Television Ltd, 19–22
Rathbone Place, London W1P 1DF
Telephone: 0171 637 6700

The Travel Channel
Landmark Travel Channel Ltd, 66
Newman Street, London W1P 3LA
Telephone: 0171 636 5401

TV Asia
TV Asia House, Spring Villa Park,
Spring Villa Road, Edgware,
Middlesex HA8 7EB
Telephone: 0181 381 2233

UK Gold
UK Gold Broadcasting Ltd, 180
Wardour Street, London W1V 4AE
Telephone: 0171 306 6100
Launched by BBC and Thames
Television in November 1992.

UK Living
The Quadrangle, 180 Wardour Street,
London W1V 4AE
Telephone: 0171 306 6100

VH1
MTV Europe, Hawley Crescent,
London NW1 8TT
Telephone: 0171 284 7777

Wire TV
United Artists Programming, Twyman
House, 16 Bonny Street, London
NW1 9PG
Telephone: 0171 813 5000

Miscellaneous TV

Focus TV
Victoria House, 62–72 Victoria Street,
St Albans, Herts AL1 3XH
Telephone: 01727 810101
Transmits a 30-minute cycle of public
information and entertainment
displayed in maternity, X-ray, accident
and emergency and other waiting
areas in hospitals throughout the UK.

Inflight Productions
3 Wedgwood Mews, Greek Street,
London W1V 5LW
Telephone: 0171 734 6747
Produces in-flight entertainment
programmes for airlines such as Virgin
Atlantic, Cathay Pacific and KLM.

ITN (Independent Television News)
200 Gray's Inn Road, London
WC1X 8XZ
Telephone: 0171 833 3000

London News Network
The London Television Centre, Upper
Ground, London SE1 9LT
Telephone: 0171 827 7700
Joint venture, co-owned by Carlton
and Granada, providing a daily news
service. Also has a sports division,
Independent Sports Network,
providing services to Carlton, LWT,
GMTV and Meridian.

SSVC Television (part of Services
Sound and Vision Corporation)
Chalfont Grove, Narcot Lane,
Chalfont St Peter, Bucks SL9 8TN
Telephone: 0171 724 1234

Teletext UK Limited
101 Farm Lane, Fulham, London
SW6 1QJ
Telephone: 0171 386 5000

Radio

BBC National Radio

BBC Radios 1, 2, 3, 4, 5 Live
Broadcasting House, Portland Place,
London W1A 1AA
Telephone: 0171 580 4468/0181 743
8000

BBC World Service
Bush House, PO Box 76, The Strand,
London WC2B 4PH
Telephone: 0171 240 3456

BBC Local Radio

Northern Ireland

BBC Radio Foyle
8 Northland Road, Londonderry
BT48 7JD
Telephone: 01504 262244

BBC Radio Ulster
Broadcasting House, Ormeau Avenue,
Belfast BT2 8HQ
Telephone: 01232 338000

Scotland

BBC Highland
7 Culduthel Road, Inverness IV2 4AD
Telephone: 01463 720720

BBC Orkney
Castle Street, Kirkwall KW15 1DF
Telephone: 01856 873939

BBC Shetland
Brentham House, Harbour Street,
Lerwick ZE1 0LR
Telephone: 01595 4747

BBC Dundee
Nethergate Centre, 66 Nethergate,
Dundee DD1 4ER
Telephone: 01382 202481

BBC Selkirk
Old Municipal Buildings, High Street,
Selkirk TD7 4BU
Telephone: 01750 21884

BBC Dumfries
Elmbank, Lovers Walk, Dumfries
DG1 1NZ
Telephone: 01387 268008

Radio Nan Gaidheal
Rosebank, 52 Church Street,
Stornoway, Isle of Lewis HS1 2LS
Telephone: 01851 705000

Wales

Radio Clwyd
The Old School House, Glanrafon
Road, Mold, Clwyd CH7 1PA
Telephone: 01352 700367

England: Midlands and East

BBC Three Counties Radio
PO Box 3CR, Hastings Street, Luton,
Bedfordshire LU1 5XL
Telephone: 01582 44100

BBC Radio Cambridgeshire
PO Box 96, Cambridge CB2 1LD
Telephone: 01223 259696

BBC CWR
25 Warwick Road, Coventry CV1 2WR
Telephone: 01203 559911

BBC Radio Derby
PO Box 269, Derby DE1 3HI
Telephone: 01332 361111

BBC Essex
198 New London Road, Chelmsford,
Essex CM2 9XB
Telephone: 01245 262393

BBC Hereford & Worcester
Hylton Road, Worcester WR2 5WW
Telephone: 01905 748485

BBC Radio Leicester
Epic House, Charles Street, Leicester
LE1 3SH
Telephone: 0116 251 6688

BBC Radio Lincolnshire
PO Box 219, Newport, Lincoln
LN1 3XY
Telephone: 01522 511411

BBC Radio Norfolk
Norfolk Tower, Surrey Street, Norwich
NR1 3PA
Telephone: 01603 617411

BBC Radio Northampton
Broadcasting House, Abington Street,
Northampton NN1 2BH
Telephone: 01604 239100

BBC Radio Nottingham
York House, Mansfield Road,
Nottingham NG1 3JB
Telephone: 0115 9550500

BBC Radio Shropshire
PO Box 397, Shrewsbury SY1 3TT
Telephone: 01743 248484

BBC Radio Stoke
Cheapside, Hanley, Stoke-on-Trent
ST1 1JJ
Telephone: 01782 208080

BBC Radio Suffolk
Broadcasting House, St Matthews
Street, Ipswich IP1 3EP
Telephone: 01473 25000

BBC Radio WM
PO Box 206, Birmingham B5 7SD
Telephone: 0121 414 8484

England: North

BBC Radio Cleveland
Broadcasting House, PO Box 95FM,
Middlesbrough TS1 5DG
Telephone: 01642 225211

BBC Radio Cumbria
Annetwell Street, Carlisle, Cumbria
CA3 8BB
Telephone: 01228 592444

BBC GMR
BBC North, Oxford Road,
Manchester M60 1SJ
Telephone: 0161 200 2000

BBC Radio Humberside
9 Chapel Street, Hull HU1 3NU
Telephone: 01482 323232

BBC Radio Lancashire
Darwen Street, Blackburn, Lancs
BB2 2EA
Telephone: 01254 262411

BBC Radio Leeds
Broadcasting House, Woodhouse
Lane, Leeds LS2 9PX
Telephone: 0113 244 2131

BBC Radio Merseyside
55 Paradise Street, Liverpool L1 3BP
Telephone: 0151 708 5500

BBC Radio Newcastle
Broadcasting Centre, Barrack Road,
Newcastle upon Tyne NE99 2NE
Telephone: 0191 232 4141

BBC Radio Sheffield
60 Westbourne Road, Sheffield
S10 2QU
Telephone: 0114 268 6185

BBC Radio York
20 Bootham Row, York YO3 7BR
Telephone: 01904 641351

England: South

BBC Radio Bristol
PO Box 194, Bristol BS99 7QT
Telephone: 0117 9741111

BBC Somerset Sound (part of Radio
Bristol)
14 Paul Street, Taunton TA1 3PF
Telephone: 01823 252437

BBC Radio Cornwall
Phoenix Wharf, Truro, Cornwall
TR1 1UA
Telephone: 01872 75421

BBC Radio Devon
Linkmail 123, Exeter, Devon
Telephone: 01392 215651

BBC Dorset FM (part of Radio
Devon)
PO Box 900, Dorchester DT1 1TP
Telephone: 01305 269654

BBC Radio Gloucestershire
London Road, Gloucester GL1 1SW
Telephone: 01452 308585

BBC GLR
35c Marylebone High Street, London
W1A 4LG
Telephone: 0171 224 2424

BBC Radio Guernsey
Commerce House, Les Banques, St
Peter Port, Guernsey GY1 2HS
Telephone: 01481 728977

BBC Radio Jersey
18 Parade Road, St Helier, Jersey
JE2 3PL
Telephone: 01534 870000

BBC Radio Kent
Sun Pier, Chatham, Kent ME4 4EZ
Telephone: 01634 830505

BBC Southern Counties Radio
Broadcasting Centre, Guildford,
Surrey GU2 5AP
Telephone: 01483 306306

BBC Radio Solent
Broadcasting House, Havelock Road,
Southampton SO14 7PW
Telephone: 01703 631311

BBC Thames Valley FM
269 Banbury Road, Summertown,
Oxford OX2 7DW
Telephone: 01865 311444

BBC Wiltshire Sound
PO Box 1234, Swindon SN1 3RW
Telephone: 01793 513626

Independent National Radio

Atlantic 252
PO Box 252, London WIE 2RA
Telephone: 0171 436 4012

Classic FM
Academic House, 24–28 Oval Road,
London NW1 7DQ
Telephone: 0171 284 3000

IRN
200 Gray's Inn Road, London
WC1X 8DP
Telephone: 0171 388 4558

Talk Radio UK
76 Oxford Street, London W1N 0TR
Telephone: 0171 636 1089

Virgin 1215
1 Golden Square, London W1R 4DJ
Telephone: 0171 434 1215

Independent Regional Radio

Century Radio
Century House, Church Street,
Gateshead, Tyne & Wear NE8 2YY
Telephone: 0191 477 6666

Galaxy Radio
25 Portland Square, Bristol BS2 8RZ
Telephone: 0117 9240111

Heart FM
PO Box 1007, 1 The Square, 111 Broad
Street, Edgbaston, Birmingham
B15 1AS
Telephone: 0121 626 1007

Heart FM
The Chrysalis Building, Bramley
Road, London W10 6SP
Telephone: 0171 468 1062

Jazz FM 100.4
The World Trade Centre, Exchange
Quay, Manchester M5 3EJ
Telephone: 0161 877 1004

Scot FM
Albert Quay, Leith EH6 7DN
Telephone: 0131 554 6677

Independent Local Radio and Community Radio Stations

Northern Ireland

96.7 BCR
Russell Court Building, Claremont
Street, Belfast BT9 6JX
Telephone: 01232 438500

Cool FM
PO Box 974, Belfast BT1 1RT
Telephone: 01247 817181

Downtown Radio
Newtownards, Co Down BT23 4ES
Telephone: 01247 815555

Q102.9
The Old Waterside Railway Station,
Duke Street, Waterside, Londonderry
BT47 1DH
Telephone: 01504 44449

Townland Radio 828 AM
PO Box 828, Cookstown, Co Tyrone
BT80 9LQ
Telephone: 016487 64828

Scotland

Radio Borders
Tweedside Park, Galashiels,
Selkirkshire TD1 3TD
Telephone: 01896 759444

Central FM
PO Box 103, Stirling FK7 7YJ
Telephone: 01786 451188

Clyde 1 FM/Clyde 2
Clydebank Business Park, Clydebank,
Glasgow G81 2RX
Telephone: 0141 306 2200

Forth FM/Max AM
Forth House, Forth Street, Edinburgh
EH1 3LF
Telephone: 0131 556 9255

Heartland FM
Lower Oakfield, Pitlochry, Perthshire
PH16 5DS
(COMMUNITY RADIO)
Telephone: 01796 474040

Moray Firth Radio
PO Box 271, Inverness IV3 6SF
Telephone: 01463 224433

Nevis Radio
Inverlochy Fort William, Inverness-
shire PH33 6LU
Telephone: 01397 700007

NE Community Radio (NECR)
Town House, The Square, Kintore,
Aberdeenshire AB51 0US
Telephone: 01467 632878

North Sound One/North Sound Two
45 King's Gate, Aberdeen AB2 6BL
Telephone: 01224 632234

Q96
26 Lady Lane, Paisley PA1 2LG
Telephone: 0141 887 9630

**SIBC (Shetland Islands
Broadcasting Corporation)**
Market Street, Lerwick, Shetland
ZE1 0JN
Telephone: 01595 695299

South West Sound
Campbell House, Bankend Road,
Dumfries DG1 4TH
Telephone: 01387 250999

Radio Tay AM/Tay FM
PO Box 123, 6 North Isla Street,
Dundee DD3 7JQ
Telephone: 01382 200800

West Sound Radio
Radio House, 54 Holmston Road, Ayr
KA7 3BE
Telephone: 01292 283662

Wales

Radio Ceredigion
The Old Welsh School, Alexandra
Road, Aberystwyth SY23 1LF
(COMMUNITY RADIO)
Telephone: 01970 627999

Radio Maldwyn
The Park, Newtown Powys SY16 2NZ
(COMMUNITY RADIO)
Telephone: 01686 623555

Marcher Coast 96.3 FM
41 Conway Road, Colwyn Bay, Clwyd
LL28 5AB
Telephone: 01492 534555

MFM
The Studios, Mold Road, Wrexham,
Clwyd LL11 4AF
Telephone: 01978 752202

Red Dragon FM
Radio House, West Canal Wharf,
Cardiff CF1 5XJ
Telephone: 01222 384041

Swansea Sound
Victoria Road, Gowerton, Swansea,
West Glamorgan SA4 3AB
Telephone: 01792 893751

Touch AM
PO Box 99, Cardiff CF1 5YJ
Telephone: 01222 237878

England: Midlands and East

BRMB 96.4 & Xtra AM
Radio House, Aston Road North,
Birmingham B6 4BZ
Telephone: 0121 359 4481

Beacon Radio & WABC
267 Tettenhall Road, Wolverhampton
WV6 0DQ
Telephone: 01902 757211

Radio Broadland
St George's Plain, 47–49 Colegate,
Norwich NR3 1DB
Telephone: 01603 630621

**Chiltern Radio & Chiltern Radio
Supergold**
Broadcast Centre, Chiltern Road,
Dunstable Beds LU6 1HQ
Telephone: 01582 666001

**B97 Chiltern FM & Chiltern Radio
Supergold (East)**
55 Goldington Road, Bedford, Beds
MK40 3LS
Telephone: 01234 272400

Choice FM
95 Broad Street, Birmingham B15 1AU
Telephone: 0121 616 1000

Classic Gold 1332 & Hereward FM
PO Box 225, Queensgate Centre,
Peterborough, PE1 1XJ
Telephone: 01733 460460

Community Radio Milton Keynes
The Broadcast Centre, 14 Vincent
Avenue, Crownhill, Milton Keynes
MK8 0AB
Telephone: 01908 265266

County Sound
The Friary Shopping Centre, High
Street, Guildford, Surrey GU1 4XX
Telephone: 01483 451964

Fox FM
Brush House, Pony Road, Cowley,
Oxford OX4 2XR
Telephone: 01865 748787

Gem AM & Radio Trent
29–31 Castle Gate, Nottingham
NG1 7AP
Telephone: 0115 952 7000

Hereward FM
See Classic Gold 1332

Horizon Radio 103.3
Broadcast Centre, 14 Vincent Avenue,
Crownhill, Milton Keynes, Bucks
MK8 0AB
Telephone: 01908 269111

KCBC
PO Box 1584, Kettering, Northants
NN16 8PU
Telephone: 01536 412413

Kix 96
2nd Floor, Ringway House, Hill Street,
Coventry CV1 4AN
Telephone: 01203 525656

KLFM 96.7
PO Box 77, 18 Blackfriars Street,
King's Lynn, Norfolk PE30 1NN
Telephone: 01553 772777

Leicester Sound
Granville House, Granville Road,
Leicester LE1 7RW
Telephone: 0116 2561300

Lincs FM
PO Box 102, Lincoln LN5 7JS
Telephone: 01522 549900

Marcher Gold & MFM
The Studios, Mold Road, Wrexham,
Clwyd LL11 4AF
Telephone: 01978 752202

Mellow 1557
The Media Centre, 2 St John's Wynd,
Culver Square, Colchester, Essex
CO1 1WQ
Telephone: 01255 675303

Mercia Classic Gold & Mercia FM
Hertford Place, Coventry CV1 3TT
Telephone: 01203 868200

**Northants Radio & Northants
Radio Supergold**
Broadcast Centre, The Enterprise
Park, Boughton Green Road,
Northampton NN2 7AH
Telephone: 01604 792411

Q103 FM
PO Box 103, The Vision Park, Histon,
Cambridge CB4 4WW
Telephone: 01223 235255

Ram FM
The Market Place, Derby DE1 3AA
Telephone: 01332 292945

Sabras Sound
Radio House, 63 Melton Road,
Leicester LE4 6PN
Telephone: 0116 2610666

SGR Colchester
PO Box 250, Colchester CO2 7DH
Telephone: 01206 575859

SGR-FM (Bury)
PO Box 250, Bury St Edmunds,
Suffolk IP33 1AD
Telephone: 01284 702622

SGR-FM (Ipswich)
Radio House, Alpha Business Park,
White House Road, Ipswich, Suffolk
IP1 5LT
Telephone: 01473 461000

Signal Gold & Signal One
Stoke Road, Stoke-on-Trent, Staffs
ST4 2SR
Telephone: 01782 747047

Supa AM
730 Pershore Road, Selly Park,
Birmingham B29 7NJ
Telephone: 0121 472 1000

Sunshine 855
Sunshine House, Waterside, Ludlow,
Shropshire SY8 1GS
Telephone: 01584 873795

Trent FM
29–31 Castle Gate, Nottingham
NG1 7AP
Telephone: 0115 9527000

WABC
See Beacon Radio

Radio Wyvern
5 & 6 Barbourne Terrace, Worcester
WR1 3JZ
Telephone: 01905 612212

Radio XL
KMS House, Bradford Street,
Birmingham B12 0JD
Telephone: 0121 753 5353

England: North

A1 FM
Radio House, 11 Woodland Road,
Darlington, Co Durham DL3 7BJ
Telephone: 01325 381032

Radio Aire FM & Magic 828
51 Burley Road, Leeds LS3 1LR
Telephone: 0113 2452299

The Bay
PO Box 969, St George's Quay,
Lancaster LA1 3LD
Telephone: 01524 848747

CFM
PO Box 964, Carlisle, Cumbria
CA1 3NG
Telephone: 0228 818964

City FM & Radio City Gold
8–10 Stanley Street, Liverpool L1 6AF
Telephone: 0151 227 5100

Fortune 1458
PO Box 1458, Quay West, Trafford
Park, Manchester M17 1FL
Telephone: 0161 872 1458

Great North Radio & Metro FM
Long Rigg Swalwell, Newcastle upon
Tyne NE99 1BB
Telephone: 0191 420 3040 (Great
North Radio)
Telephone: 0191 420 0971 (Metro FM)

Great Yorkshire Gold
Radio House, 900 Herries Road,
Sheffield S6 1RH
Telephone: 0114 2852121

Hallam FM
Radio House, 900 Herries Road,
Sheffield S6 1RH
Telephone: 0114 2853333

Kiss 102
Kiss House, PO Box 102, Manchester
M60 1GJ
Telephone: 0161 228 0102

Magic 828
See Radio Aire

Manx Radio
Broadcasting House, PO Box 1368,
Douglas, Isle of Man IM99 1SW
Telephone: 01624 661066

Metro FM
See Great North Radio

Minster FM
PO Box 123, Dunnington, York
YO1 5ZX
Telephone: 01904 488878

MFM
See Marcher Gold

Piccadilly Gold & Piccadilly Key 103
127–131 The Piazza, Piccadilly Plaza,
Manchester M1 4AW
Telephone: 0161 236 9913

The Pulse
Pennine House, PO Box 3000, Forster
Square, Bradford BD1 5NE
Telephone: 01274 731521

Radio Wave
965 Mowbry Drive, Blackpool, Lancs
FY3 7JR
Telephone: 01253 304965

**Red Rose Gold & Red Rose Rock
FM**
PO Box 999, St Pauls Square, Preston
PR1 1YE
Telephone: 01772 556301

Signal Cheshire
Regent House, Heaton Lane,
Stockport SK4 1BX
Telephone: 0161 480 5445

Stray FM
Stray Studios, PO Box 972, Station
Parade, Harrogate HG1 5YF
Telephone: 01423 522972

Sun City 103.4
PO Box 1034, Sunderland, SR1 3YZ
Telephone: 0191 567 3333

Sunrise FM
Sunrise House, 30 Chapel Street, Little
Germany, Bradford BD1 5DN
Telephone: 01274 735043

TFM Radio
Radio House, Yale Crescent,
Thornaby, Stockton-on-Tees,
Cleveland TS17 6AA
Telephone: 01642 615111

Viking FM
Commercial Road, Hull HU1 2SG
Telephone: 01482 325141

Yorkshire Coast Radio
PO Box 962, Scarborough, North
Yorkshire YO12 5YX
Telephone: 01723 500962

England: South

210 Classic Gold & 2-Ten FM
The Chase, Calcot, Reading, Berks
RG31 7RZ
Telephone: 01734 455210

2CR Classic Gold & 2CR FM
517 Southcote Road, Bournemouth
BH1 3LR
Telephone: 01202 294881

Boss 603 Radio
Churchill Studios, Churchill Road,
Cheltenham, Gloucestershire
GL53 7EP
Telephone: 01242 255023

Breeze
See Essex FM

Brunel Classic Gold
PO Box 2000, Bristol BS99 7SN
Telephone: 0117 9843201
and PO Box 2000, Swindon SN4 7EX
Telephone: 01793 440301

Capital FM & Capital Gold
Euston Tower, Euston Road, London
NW1 3DR
Telephone: 0171 608 6080

Channel 103 FM
6 Tunnel Street, St Helier, Jersey
JE2 4LU
Telephone: 01534 888103

Channel Travel Radio
UK Terminal, PO Box 2000,
Folkestone, Kent CT18 8XY
Telephone: 01303 272222

Choice FM
16–18 Trinity Gardens, London
SW9 8DP
Telephone: 0171 738 7969

Country 1035
PO Box 1035, London SW6 3QQ
Telephone: 0171 384 1175

Eleven Seventy AM
PO Box 1170, High Wycombe
HP13 6YT
Telephone: 01494 446611

Essex FM & Breeze FM
Radio House, 19–20 Clifftown Road,
Southend-on-Sea, Essex SS1 1SX
Telephone: 01702 333711

Fox FM
Brush House, Pony Road, Oxford
OX4 2XR
Telephone: 01865 748787

Gemini AM/FM
Hawthorn House, Exeter Business
Park, Exeter EX1 3QS
Telephone: 01392 444444

Gold Radio
Longmead, Shaftesbury, Dorset
SP7 8QQ
Telephone: 01747 855711

GWR FM (East)
PO Box 2000, Swindon SN4 7EX
Telephone: 01793 440300

GWR FM (West)
PO Box 2000, Bristol BS99 7SN
Telephone: 0117 9843200

Island FM
12 Westerbrook, St Sampsons,
Guernsey GY2 4QQ
Telephone: 01481 42000

Invicta FM & Invicta Supergold
Radio House, John Wilson Business
Park, Whitstable, Kent CT5 3QX
Telephone: 01227 772004

Isle of Wight Radio
119 High Street, Newport, Isle of
Wight PO30 1TP
Telephone: 01983 822557

Jazz FM 102.2
Golden Rose House, 26/27
Castlereagh Street, London W1H 6DJ
Telephone: 0171 706 4100

Kiss 100 FM
Kiss House, 80 Holloway Road,
London N7 JG
Telephone: 0171 700 6100

KFM
1 East Street, Tonbridge, Kent TN9 1AR
Telephone: 01732 369200

Lantern FM
The Light House, Market Place,
Bideford, North Devon EX39 2DR
Telephone: 01237 424444

London Greek Radio
Florentia Village, Vale Road, London
N4 1TD
Telephone: 0181 800 8001

**London News Radio & London
News Talk**
72 Hammersmith Road, London
W14 8YE
Telephone: 0171 973 1152

London Turkish Radio
185B High Road, Wood Green,
London N22 6BA
Telephone: 0181 881 0606

Melody Radio
180 Brompton Road, London SW3 1HF
Telephone: 0171 581 1054

**Radio Mercury FM (East) and
Mercury Extra AM**
Broadfield House, Brighton Road,
Crawley, West Sussex RH11 9TT
Telephone: 01293 519161
(replaced by Surrey & North East
Hampshire Radio from April 1996)

Mix 96
11 Bourbon Street, Aylesbury, Bucks
HP20 2PZ
Telephone: 01296 399396

Oasis
The Broadcast Centre, 7 Hatfield
Road, St Albans, Hertfordshire AL1 3RS
Telephone: 01727 831966

Ocean FM
Radio House, Fareham, Hampshire
PO15 5SH
Telephone: 01489 589911

Orchard FM
Haygrove House, Shoreditch,
Taunton, Somerset TA3 7BT
Telephone: 01823 338448

Pirate FM 102
Carn Brea Studios, Wilson Way,
Redruth, Cornwall TR15 3XX
Telephone: 01209 314400

Plymouth Sound
Earl's Acre, Plymouth PL3 4HX
Telephone: 01752 227272

Power FM
Radio House, Fareham, Hampshire
PO15 5SH
Telephone: 01489 589911

Premier Radio
7th Floor, Glen House, Stag Place,
London SW1E 5AG
Telephone: 0171 233 6705

RTM
Company Offices, Harrow Manor
Way, Thamesmead South, London
SE2 9XH
(COMMUNITY RADIO)
Telephone: 0181 311 3112

**Severn Sound & Severn Sound
Supergold**
Broadcast Centre, Southgate Street,
Gloucester GL1 2BR
Telephone: 01452 423791

South Coast Radio
Radio House, PO Box 2000, Brighton
BN41 2SS
Telephone: 01273 430111
and
Radio House, Fareham, Hampshire
PO15 5SH
Telephone: 01489 589911

Southern FM
Radio House, Fareham, Hampshire
PO15 5SH
Telephone: 01489 589911

Spectrum Radio 558
PO Box 5555, Brent Cross, London
NW2 1JT
Telephone: 0181 905 5000

Spire FM
City Hall Studios, Malthouse
Lane, Salisbury, Wilts
SP2 7QQ
Telephone: 01722 416644

Star FM
The Observatory Shopping Centre,
Slough, Berkshire SL1 1LH
Telephone: 01753 551066

Sunrise Radio
Sunrise House, Southall, Middlesex
UB2 4AU
Telephone: 0181 574 6666
Ten 17 (part of Essex FM)
Latton Bush Centre, Southern Way,
Harlow, Essex CM18 7BU
Telephone: 01279 432415

London Turkish Radio
93 Westbury Avenue, Wood Green,
London N22 6SQ
Telephone: 0181 881 0606

Viva!
Golden Rose House, 26–27
Castlereagh Street, London W1H 6DJ
Telephone: 0171 706 9963

Virgin Radio London
1 Golden Square, London W1R 4DJ
Telephone: 0171 434 1215

Wessex FM
Radio House, Trinity Street,
Dorchester, Dorset DT1 1DJ
Telephone: 01305 250333

Wey Valley 102
Prospect Place, Mill Lane, Alton,
Hampshire GU34 2SY
Telephone: 01420 544444

Retail Radio Services

Asda FM (satellite)
PO Box 100, Tyldesley, Manchester
M29 7TT
Telephone: 01942 896111

Fashion FM (cable)
36–38 Great Castle Street, London
W1N 7AB
Telephone: 0171 927 0226

Retail Broadcasting Services
29/30 Windmill Street, London
W1P 1HG
Telephone: 0171 580 0444
Provides radio services to Granada,
Texas and BhS.

Miscellaneous Radio

BFBS (British Forces Broadcasting Service)
PO Box 1234, London W2 1XN
Telephone: 0171 724 1234

The Radio Authority's (see Chapter 10) annual pocket book includes contacts for cable and satellite radio services.

Broadcast News Agencies

Independent Radio News (IRN)
200 Gray's Inn Road, London WC1X 8XZ
Telephone: 0171 388 4558
Part of ITN Radio; supplies bulletins and other news material to most independent radio stations.

Network News
Chiltern Road, Dunstable, Beds LU6 1HQ
Telephone: 01582 666884
Provides national and international news for INR and ILR.

Reuters Television and Radio News
200 Gray's Inn Road, London WC1X 8XZ
Telephone: 0171 510 5495/388 4558

Supplies news to the two London stations owned by Reuters (London News and London News Talk) and to a few other independent radio stations, including Virgin.

Sportsmedia Broadcasting
47 Canalot Production Studios, 222 Kensal Road, London W10 5BN
Telephone: 0181 962 9000
Provides UK and international sports news for INR and ILR.

WTN (Worldwide Television News)
The Interchange, 32 Oval Road, Camden Lock, London NW1 7EP
Telephone: 0171 410 5200

Chapter 13 / Useful Addresses (4)
Major Publishing
Houses

There are many publishing houses in the UK; here are just some of the more established ones. You'll find a fuller list in *Writers' & Artists' Yearbook* or *The Writers' Handbook*. Under each company we've given a brief idea of the main subject areas in which each one specializes.

AA Publishing
The Automobile Association, Fanum House, Basingstoke, Hampshire RG21 4EA
Telephone: 01256 491574
Travel guidebooks, maps and atlases.

BT Batsford Ltd
4 Fitzhardinge Street, London W1H 0AH
Telephone: 0171 486 8484
Horticulture, needlework, architecture, art techniques and crafts.

BBC Books (inc. Network Books)
BBC Worldwide, Woodlands, 80 Wood Lane, London W12 0TT
Telephone: 0181 743 5588/576 2000
TV tie-ins and children's books.

Berlitz Publishing Co Ltd
Berlitz House, Peterley Road, Oxford OX4 2TX
Telephone: 01865 747033
Travel and languages.

A & C Black (Publishers) Ltd
35 Bedford Row, London WC1R 4JH
Telephone: 0171 242 0946
Sports, travel, childen and dance. Also includes Christopher Helm imprint, specializing in travel guides.

Blackwell Publishers
108 Cowley Road, Oxford OX4 1JF
Telephone: 01865 791100
Academic books.

Bloomsbury Publishing plc
2 Soho Square, London W1V 6HB
Telephone: 0171 494 2111
Literary fiction and non-fiction.

Boxtree
2nd Floor, Broadwall House, 21 Broadwall, London SE1 9PL
Telephone: 0171 928 9696
TV tie-ins.

Butterworth & Co (Publishers) Ltd
(inc. Butterworth-Heinemann and
Focal Press)
Halsbury House, 35 Chancery Lane,
London WC2A 1EL
Telephone: 0171 400 2500
Tax and legal books; medical and
technical.

Cadogan Books Ltd
London House, Parkgate Road,
London SW11 4NQ
Telephone: 0171 738 1961
Travel and chess.

Cambridge University Press
The Edinburgh Building, Shaftesbury
Road, Cambridge CB2 2RU
Telephone: 01223 312393
Academic.

Cassell plc
Wellington House, 125 Strand, London
WC2R 0BB
Telephone: 0171 420 5555
Imprints include Blandford Press
(natural history); Studio Vista
(practical arts, art, film); Stirling (crafts
and woodwork); Lark (crafts); Millner
(crafts); Cassell (reference; food and
wine, art and architecture); Gollancz
(current affairs; fiction); Mansell
(religious); Ward Lock (gardening; food
and wine).

Chapman & Hall Ltd (inc. Blackie
Academic and Professional, Blueprint)
2–6 Boundary Row, London SE1 8HN
Telephone: 0171 865 0066
Scientific, academic and medical.

Consumers' Association
2 Marylebone Road, London NW1 4DF
Telephone: 0171 830 6000
Consumer-related information and
reference books.

David & Charles Publishers
Brunel House, Horde Close, Newton
Abbot, Devon TQ12 4PU
Telephone: 01626 61121
Hobby books.

Andre Deutsch Ltd
106 Great Russell Street, London
WC1B 3LJ
Telephone: 0171 580 2746
Fiction, biography and art.

Dorling Kindersley Ltd
9 Henrietta Street, Covent Garden,
London WC2E 8PS
Telephone: 0171 836 5411
Non-fiction, encyclopaedias and travel
guides.

Faber & Faber Ltd
3 Queen Square, London WC1N 3AU
Telephone: 0171 465 0045
Literary fiction, poetry.

Fourth Estate
6 Salem Road, London W2 4BU
Telephone: 0171 727 8993
Literary fiction. Imprints include:
Blueprint (architecture); Guardian
(non-fiction, reference, media guides).

Granta Publications Ltd
2/3 Hanover Yard, Noel Road,
Islington, London N1 8BE
Telephone: 0171 704 9776
Travel journals and fiction.

Guinness Publishing Ltd
33 London Road, Enfield, Middlesex
EN2 6DJ
Telephone: 0181 367 4567
Factual.

HarperCollins Publishers
77–85 Fulham Palace Road,
Hammersmith, London W6 8JB
Telephone: 0181 741 7070
Imprints include: George Allen &
Unwin (educational); Aquarian Press
(self-help); Armada (children's fiction);
Cartographic (maps); Flamingo
(general consumer non-fiction); Lions
(children); Nicholson (maps); Pandora
(general non-fiction); Thorsons (self-
help).

Hobsons Publishing plc
Bateman Street, Cambridge CB2 1LZ
Telephone: 01223 354551
Educational.

Hodder Headline plc
338 Euston Road, London NW1 3BH
Telephone: 0171 837 6000
Imprints include: Headline (fiction);
Hodder & Stoughton (general);
Sceptre (literary fiction); Coronet
(paperbacks); New English Library
(fiction, horror, thrillers, fantasy);
Hodder & Stoughton Educational
(religious and children's); Arnold
(history books, non-fiction and
technical).

Kogan Page Ltd
120 Pentonville Road, London N1 9JN
Telephone: 0171 278 0433
Business, transport and education;
careers.

Larousse plc
Elsley House, 24–30 Great Titchfield
Street, London W1P 7AD
Telephone: 0171 631 0878
Imprints include: Chambers
(reference); Harrap (foreign languages);
Kingfisher (children's).

**Little, Brown and Company (UK)
Ltd**
Brettenham House, Lancaster Place,
London WC2E 7EN
Telephone: 0171 911 8000
Imprints include: Abacus (paperback,
travel); Orbit (science fiction); Warner
(romantic); Warner-Futura (fiction and
non-fiction).

Longman Group Ltd (inc. various
Longman imprints)
Longman House, Burnt Mill, Harlow,
Essex CM20 2JE
Telephone: 01279 426721
Teaching books.

Macmillan Publishers Ltd
25 Eccleston Place, London SW1W 9NF
Telephone: 0171 836 6633
Imprints include Pan (general fiction,
non-fiction and children's); Macmillan
(general fiction, non-fiction, children's,
travel and Macmillan Academic and
Macmillan Reference); Picador and
Papermac (literary fiction and non-
fiction); Sidgwick & Jackson (music,
biographies and history); Michael
O'Mara (humour, biographies, history,
novelty, children's); St Martin's Press
(general fiction, non-fiction, westerns,
horror, film tie-ins); TOR (fantasy and
science fiction); Macmillan Caribbean
(cookery, children's, literature and
poetry, history, maps and atlases).

Manchester University Press
Oxford Road, Manchester M13 9NR
Telephone: 0161 273 5539
Academic and educational.

The Orion Publishing Group Ltd
Orion House, 5 Upper St Martin's
Lane, London WC2H 9EA
Telephone: 0171 240 3444
Imprints include: Everyman (classics);
Phoenix (offbeat/first novelists); Orion
(commercial); Weidenfeld & Nicolson
(serious fiction and general fiction);
Millennium (science fiction).

Oxford University Press
Walton Street, Oxford OX2 6DP
Telephone: 01865 56767
Academic.

Pavilion Books
26 Upper Ground, London SE1 9PD
Telephone: 0171 620 1666
Gardening and cookery, coffee table
books.

Penguin Books Ltd
27 Wrights Lane, London W8 5TZ
Telephone: 0171 416 3000
Imprints include Arkana (new age,
mystic); Blackie Children's Books;
Signet (fiction and non-fiction);
DragonLance/Fighting Fantasy/Roc
(all science fiction and science fantasy);
Frederick Warne (children's); Penguin
(non-academic fiction and non-fiction);
Puffin (paperback, children's fiction
and non-fiction); Pelham (sporting,
leisure, pets); Buildings of England
(architecture); Michael Joseph Ltd
(hardback non-fiction and fiction);
Hamish Hamilton/Viking (adult and
children's hardback non-fiction and
fiction).

Piatkus Books
5 Windmill Street, London W1P 1HF
Telephone: 0171 631 0710
Mind, body and spirit; cookery;
business; romantic fiction.

Quartet Books Ltd
27 Goodge Street, London W1P 2LD
Telephone: 0171 636 3992
General fiction and non-fiction.

Random House UK Ltd
20 Vauxhall Bridge Road, London
SW1V 2SA
Telephone: 0171 973 9670
Imprints include: Fodor (travel); Red
Fox (children's); Jonathan Cape/
Chatto & Windus/Vintage (literary
fiction); Hutchinson (general fiction,
adult and children); Arrow Books (mass
market fiction and non-fiction); Ebury
Press (craft and cookery); Vermilion
(health, new age); Century (mass
market literature); Random House
Audio Books.

Reader's Digest Association Ltd
Berkeley Square House, Berkeley
Square, London W1X 6AB
Telephone: 0171 629 8144
Cookbooks, gardening, general
reference.

Reed International Books
Michelin House, 81 Fulham Road,
London SW3 6RB
Telephone: 0171 581 9393
Mandarin/Methuen (children's);
Minerva (fiction); Mitchell Beazley
(illustrated books, cookery); Secker &
Warburg/Sinclair-Stevenson (non-
academic fiction and non-fiction);
Butterworths (law); Conran Octopus
(coffee-table books); Hamlyn (non-
fiction illustrated guides e.g. gardening

and cooking); William Heinemann
(education and consumer guides);
Heinemann Young Books (children's
reference); Butterworth Heinemann
(medical and business).

Routledge
11 New Fetter Lane, London EC4P 4EE
Telephone: 0171 583 9855
Academic textbooks.

Simon & Schuster (inc. Pocket Books, Touchstone)
West Garden Place, Kendal Street,
London W2 2AQ
Telephone: 0171 724 7577
Fiction and non-fiction.

SPCK (Society for Promoting Christian Knowledge)
Holy Trinity Church, Marylebone
Road, London NW1 4DU
Telephone: 0171 387 5282
Theology and (under Sheldon Press
imprint) self-help.

Thames and Hudson Ltd
30–34 Bloomsbury Street, London
WC1B 3QP
Telephone: 0171 636 5488
Non-fiction, travel, fashion, art, design
and crafts.

Transworld Publishers Ltd
61–63 Uxbridge Road, Ealing, London
W5 5SA
Telephone: 0181 579 2652

Mass-market publishers. Imprints
include: Bantam and Corgi (mass-
market fiction and non-fiction); Black
Swan (literary fiction); Partridge
(hardback sport); Doubleday
(hardback non-fiction, cookery
and biographies).

Virago Press
20 Vauxhall Bridge Road, London
SW1V 2SA
Telephone: 0171 973 9750
Mostly feminist fiction and non-fiction.

Virgin Publishing Ltd
332 Ladbroke Grove, London W10 5AH
Telephone: 0181 968 7554
Black Lace (erotic fiction for women);
Nexus (erotic fiction for men); Virgin
Publishing (biographies, sport and
film).

Walker Books Ltd
87 Vauxhall Walk, London SE11 5HJ
Telephone: 0171 793 0909
Children's.

The Women's Press
34 Great Sutton Street, London
EC1V 0DX
Telephone: 0171 251 3007
Women's literature.

Chapter 14 / **Trade Publications**

Trade publications are an invaluable way of getting a feel for the field and an awareness of the issues affecting it. It would be too costly to buy all of these magazines regularly but your local library may have a subscription.

AM/FM
Monthly, £2.95 (annual UK sub, £30). News and features for people working in or associated with the UK and European radio broadcast industry. Carries a little recruitment advertising. Published by Glasgow Country Radio Ltd. (Telephone: 0141 333 1054)

Ariel
Weekly. Free to BBC staff; otherwise, £26 for a six-month subscription; £50 for a year. BBC staff journal, with news and features on what's happening in the Corporation, plus lots of recruitment ads (though most of these are also advertised externally). Published by the BBC. (Telephone: 0171 765 3623)

The Bookseller
Weekly, £1.95. Trade newspaper for the book business, with news and features on the industry and forthcoming titles. Published by J Whitaker & Sons Ltd. (Telephone: 0171 836 8911)

Broadcast
Weekly, £1.80. Carries a large selection of radio and television job ads. Published by EMAP Business Communications. (Telephone: 0171 837 1212)

Cable and Satellite Europe
Monthly; annual subscription, £70. Carries news and features on the cable and satellite industry around the world. Published by 21st Century Business Publications Ltd. (Telephone: 0171 351 3612)

Campaign
Weekly, £1.70. Trade magazine for the advertising industry but carries some straight media-related stories. Carries recruitment advertising but not for journalism jobs. Published by Haymarket Campaign Publications Ltd. (Telephone: 0171 402 4200)

Creative Review
Monthly, £2.95. Journal reflecting the television and commercials business. Carries job ads. (Telephone: 0171 439 4222)

The Freelance

Bi-monthly news-sheet, free to freelance membes of the NUJ, covering issues of concern to freelances. Published by the NUJ. (Telephone: 0171 278 7916)

Media Week

Weekly, £1.70 (annual subscription, £85). Aimed largely at the advertising side of the industry but has news and features on matters of editorial interest too. Carries recruitment ads for publishing and sales jobs. Published by EMAP Business Communications Ltd. (Telephone: 0171 505 8000)

Publishing News

Weekly, £1.50 (annual sub, £70). Magazine for people working in the book trade, with news and details of forthcoming titles. Limited recruitment advertising. Published by Publishing News. (Telephone: 0171 404 0304)

The Radio Magazine

Weekly; annual subscription £60 (available on subscription only). Carries recruitment ads for independent radio. Published by Goldcrest Broadcasting Ltd. (Telephone: 01536 418558)

SPREd Magazine

Quarterly magazine of the Society of Picture Researchers & Editors. Annual UK sub, £25. (Telephone: 0171 431 9886)

Stage & Television Today

Weekly, 70p. Although it mostly runs ads for jobs in the theatre, it's also good for TV vacancies; you will probably need to order it specially from your newsagent; published by Carson & Comerford Ltd. (Telephone: 0171 403 1818)

Stage, Screen and Radio

Published ten times a year. Free to members of the Broadcasting Entertainment Cinematograph and Theatre Union (BECTU) otherwise £1.50 (annual sub in UK £16). News and issues affecting the broadcast industry, largely on the technical side. No recruitment ads. Published by BECTU. (Telephone: 0171 437 8506)

Television

Ten issues a year. Free to members of the Royal Television Society (RTS); otherwise annual sub is £60 in the UK. News and features on TV. No recruitment advertising. Published by the RTS. (Telephone: 0171 430 1000)

TV World

Monthly, £3.95 (annual sub in UK, £50). News and features on television around the world, concentrating on international programme sales and distribution. No recruitment ads. Published by EMAP Media Ltd. (Telephone: 0171 837 1212)

Press Gazette

Weekly, £1.50. The main trade publication for print journalists. Carries a range of recruitment ads for jobs in both national and regional press. Published by EMAP Media Ltd. (Telephone: 01732 770823)

Chapter 15 / **Further Reading**

Remember that books can date quickly, particularly in such a fast-moving industry, so always check the publication date. If it's some years ago, either look for something more recent or make allowance for changes since it was published.

Journalism – general/reference

The first two books on this list are valuable handbooks. They contain names of all the major newspapers, magazines, TV companies, etc., plus information on literary prizes, copyrights, preparation of typescripts, tax and social security for writers, and much more. Of the remaining books some are obviously too expensive to buy but should be available in the reference section of a good library.

Writers' & Artists' Yearbook (A & C Black, £10.99).
The Writer's Handbook (Macmillan, General Books, £12.99).
The Media Guide 1996, edited by Steve Peak (Fourth Estate, a Guardian book, £12.99).
The Reuters Handbook for Journalists, compiled by Ian Macdowall (Focal Press, £14.95).
Hart's Rules for Compositors and Readers (Oxford University Press, £9.99).
McNae's Essential Law for Journalists, edited by Tom Welsh and Walter Greenwood (Butterworths, £14.95).
Benn's Media Directory (3 vols: I UK; II Europe; III World).
Willings Press Guide (annual handbook). Includes details of newspapers, periodicals, publishers, etc.

BRAD (British Rate and Data). Huge monthly publication, published in three volumes, listing key contacts for all UK media which carry advertising (including newspapers, periodicals and broadcast media).

UK Publishers Directory, edited by Ellen Rocco (Gale Research International, £55).

Print Journalism

Careers in Journalism, Peter Medina and Vivien Donald (Kogan Page, 6th edition; £6.99).

Inside Magazines, Michael Barnard (Blueprint, £9.99).

How to Be a Freelance Journalist, Christine Hall (How To Books, £8.99).

The Freelance Journalist: How to Survive and Succeed, Christopher Dobson (Focal Press, £14.95).

Practical Newspaper Reporting, Geoffrey Harris and David Spark (Focal Press, 2nd edition, £16.95).

Subediting: A Handbook of Modern Newspaper Editing and Production, F W Hodgson (Focal Press, £14.95).

The Simple Subs Book, Leslie Sellers (Pergamon Press, £13).

Writing Feature Articles: A Practical Guide to Methods and Markets, Brendan Hennessy (Focal Press, £16.95).

Journalism for Beginners, Joan Clayton (Piatkus, £15).

Waterhouse on Newspaper Style, Keith Waterhouse (Penguin, £5.99).

Picture Researcher's Handbook, Hilary and Mary Evans (Blueprint, £39).

Writing for Magazines, Jill Dick (A & C Black £9.99).

Freelance Writing for Newspapers, Jill Dick (A & C Black £9.99).

The Way to Write Magazine Articles, John Hines (Hamish Hamilton £8.99).

Magazine Journalism Today, Anthony Davis (Focal Press, £16.99).

Modern Newspaper Practice, F W Hodgson (Focal Press, £14.99).

Broadcast Journalism

Careers in Television and Radio, Michael Selby (Kogan Page, 5th edition, £6.99).

Lights Camera Action! Careers in Film, Television and Video, Josephine Langham (BFI 1993, £9.99).

European Television Directory (NTC Publications). (Contains contacts for Euro TV stations; too pricey to buy at £68 but ask in your library).

BFI Film and Television Handbook 1995. An annual handbook with lots of useful addresses and information in it (BFI, 1996 edition, £14.99).

The Official ITV Careers Handbook (Hodder Education, 2nd edition, £9.99). 1992 edition and not updated since so probably a bit out of date but still includes valid information on job descriptions and advice.

How to Get into Films & TV, Robert Angell (How To Books, 2nd edition, £8.99).

How to Get into Radio, Bernie Simmons (How To Books, £8.99).

Broadcast Journalism: Techniques of Radio & TV News, Andrew Boyd (Focal Press, 3rd edition 1994, £17.95).

Local Radio Journalism, Paul Chantler and Sim Harris (Focal Press, £12.95).

Book Publishing

Basic Editing: The Text and *Basic Editing: The Exercises*, Nicola Harris (BHTC, £20 and £7.50).

Book Commissioning and Acquisition, Gill Davies (Blueprint, £19.99).

Careers in Publishing and Bookselling, June Lines (Kogan Page, 2nd edition, £6.99).

Copy Editing, Judith Butcher (Cambridge University Press, 3rd edition, £22.95).

A History of British Publishing, John Feather (Routledge, £12.99).

Inside Book Publishing, Giles Clark (Blueprint, 2nd edition, £12.95).

Publishing Now, edited by Peter Owen (Peter Owen, £12.95).

UK Publishers Directory edited by Ellen Rocco (Gale Research International, £60).

Directory of Publishing Volume 1: United Kingdom (annual, Cassell).

Multimedia, Tony Feldman (Blueprint, £14.99).

The Blueprint Dictionary of Printing and Publishing, John Peacock and Michael Barnard (Blueprint, £27.50).

READ MORE IN PENGUIN

READ MORE IN PENGUIN

A CHOICE OF NON-FICTION

Citizens Simon Schama

'The most marvellous book I have read about the French Revolution in the last fifty years' – *The Times*. 'He has chronicled the vicissitudes of that world with matchless understanding, wisdom, pity and truth, in the pages of this huge and marvellous book' – *Sunday Times*

1945: The World We Fought For Robert Kee

Robert Kee brings to life the events of this historic year as they unfolded, using references to contemporary newspapers, reports and broadcasts, and presenting the reader with the most vivid, immediate account of the year that changed the world. 'Enthralling ... an entirely realistic revelation about the relationship between war and peace' – *Sunday Times*

Cleared for Take-Off Dirk Bogarde

'It begins with his experiences in the Second World War as an interpreter of reconnaissance photographs ... he witnessed the liberation of Belsen – though about this he says he cannot write. But his awareness of the horrors as well as the dottiness of war is essential to the tone of this affecting and strangely beautiful book' – *Daily Telegraph*

Nine Parts of Desire Geraldine Brooks
The Hidden World of Islamic Women

'She takes us behind the veils and into the homes of women in every corner of the Middle East ... It is in her description of her meetings – like that with Khomeini's widow Khadija, who paints him as a New Man (and one for whom she dyed her hair vamp-red) – that the book excels' – *Observer*. 'Frank, engaging and captivating' – *New Yorker*

Insanely Great Steven Levy

The Apple Macintosh revolutionized the world of personal computing – yet the machinations behind its conception were nothing short of insane. 'One of the great stories of the computing industry ... a cast of astonishing characters' – *Observer*. 'Fascinating edge-of-your-seat story' – *Sunday Times*

READ MORE IN PENGUIN

A CHOICE OF NON-FICTION

Time Out Film Guide   Edited by John Pym

The definitive, up-to-the-minute directory of every aspect of world cinema from classics and silent epics to reissues and the latest releases.

Flames in the Field   Rita Kramer

During July 1944, four women agents met their deaths at Struthof-Natzweiler concentration camp at the hands of the SS. They were members of the Special Operations Executive, sent to Nazi-occupied France in 1943. *Flames in the Field* reveals that the odds against their survival were weighted even more heavily than they could possibly have contemplated, for their network was penetrated by double agents and security was dangerously lax.

Colored People   Henry Louis Gates Jr.

'A wittily drawn portrait of a semi-rural American community, in the years when racial segregation was first coming under legal challenge ... In the most beautiful English ... he recreates a past to which, in every imaginable sense, there is no going back' – *Mail on Sunday*

Naturalist   Edward O. Wilson

'His extraordinary drive, encyclopaedic knowledge and insatiable curiosity shine through on virtually every page' – *Sunday Telegraph*. 'There are wonderful accounts of his adventures with snakes, a gigantic ray, butterflies, flies and, of course, ants ... a fascinating insight into a great mind' – *Guardian*

Roots Schmoots   Howard Jacobson

'This is no exercise in sentimental journeys. Jacobson writes with a rare wit and the book sparkles with his gritty humour ... he displays a deliciously caustic edge in his analysis of what is wrong, and right, with modern Jewry' – *Mail on Sunday*

READ MORE IN PENGUIN

A CHOICE OF NON-FICTION

Mornings in the Dark   Edited by David Parkinson
The Graham Greene Film Reader

Prompted by 'a sense of fun' and 'that dangerous third Martini' at a party in June 1935, Graham Greene volunteered himself as the *Spectator* film critic. 'His film reviews are among the most trenchant, witty and memorable one is ever likely to read' – *Sunday Times*

Real Lives, Half Lives   Jeremy Hall

The world has been 'radioactive' for a hundred years – providing countless benefits to medicine and science – but there is a downside to the human mastery of nuclear physics. *Real Lives, Half Lives* uncovers the bizarre and secret stories of people who have been exposed, in one way or another, to radioactivity across the world.

Hidden Lives   Margaret Forster

'A memoir of Forster's grandmother and mother which reflects on the changes in women's lives – about sex, family, work – across three generations. It is a moving, evocative account, passionate in its belief in progress, punchy as a detective novel in its story of Forster's search for her grandmother's illegitimate daughter. It also shows how biography can challenge our basic assumptions about which lives have been significant and why' – *Financial Times*

Eating Children   Jill Tweedie

'Jill Tweedie re-creates in fascinating detail the scenes and conditions that shaped her, scarred her, broke her up or put her back together ... a remarkable story' – *Vogue*. 'A beautiful and courageous book' – Maya Angelou

The Lost Heart of Asia   Colin Thubron

'Thubron's journey takes him through a spectacular, talismanic geography of desert and mountain ... a whole glittering, terrible and romantic history lies abandoned along with thoughts of more prosperous times' – *The Times*

READ MORE IN PENGUIN

A CHOICE OF NON-FICTION

The Pillars of Hercules   Paul Theroux

At the gateway to the Mediterranean lie the two Pillars of Hercules. Beginning his journey in Gibraltar, Paul Theroux travels the long way round – through the ravaged developments of the Costa del Sol, into Corsica and Sicily and beyond – to Morocco's southern pillar. 'A terrific book, full of fun as well as anxiety, of vivid characters and curious experiences' – *The Times*

Where the Girls Are   Susan J. Douglas

In this brilliantly researched and hugely entertaining examination of women and popular culture, Susan J. Douglas demonstrates the ways in which music, TV, books, advertising, news and film have affected women of her generation. Essential reading for cultural critics, feminists and everyone else who has ever ironed their hair or worn a miniskirt.

Journals: 1954–1958   Allen Ginsberg

These pages open with Ginsberg at the age of twenty-eight, penniless, travelling alone and unknown in California. Yet, by July 1958 he was returning from Paris to New York as the poet who, with Jack Kerouac, led and inspired the Beats ...

The New Spaniards   John Hooper

Spain has become a land of extraordinary paradoxes in which traditional attitudes and contemporary preoccupations exist side by side. The country attracts millions of visitors – yet few see beyond the hotels and resorts of its coastline. John Hooper's fascinating study brings to life the many faces of Spain in the 1990s.

A Tuscan Childhood   Kinta Beevor

Kinta Beevor was five when she fell in love with her parents' castle facing the Carrara mountains. 'The descriptions of the harvesting and preparation of food and wine by the locals could not be bettered ... alive with vivid characters' – *Observer*

READ MORE IN PENGUIN

BUSINESS AND ECONOMICS

North and South David Smith

'This authoritative study ... gives a very effective account of the incredible centralization of decision-making in London, not just in government and administration, but in the press, communications and the management of every major company' – *New Statesman & Society*

I am Right – You are Wrong Edward de Bono

Edward de Bono expects his ideas to outrage conventional thinkers, yet time has been on his side, and the ideas that he first put forward twenty years ago are now accepted mainstream thinking. Here, in this brilliantly argued assault on outmoded thought patterns, he calls for nothing less than a New Renaissance.

Lloyds Bank Small Business Guide Sara Williams

This long-running guide to making a success of your small business deals with real issues in a practical way. 'As comprehensive an introduction to setting up a business as anyone could need' – *Daily Telegraph*

The *Economist* Economics Rupert Pennant-Rea and Clive Crook

Based on a series of 'briefs' published in the *Economist*, this is a clear and accessible guide to the key issues of today's economics for the general reader.

The Rise and Fall of Monetarism David Smith

Now that even Conservatives have consigned monetarism to the scrap heap of history, David Smith draws out the unhappy lessons of a fundamentally flawed economic experiment, driven by a doctrine that for years had been regarded as outmoded and irrelevant.

Understanding Organizations Charles B. Handy

Of practical as well as theoretical interest, this book shows how general concepts can help solve specific organizational problems.

READ MORE IN PENGUIN

BUSINESS AND ECONOMICS

The Affluent Society   John Kenneth Galbraith

Classical economics was born in a harsh world of mass poverty, and it has left us with a set of preoccupations hard to adapt to the realities of our own richer age. Our unfamiliar problems need a new approach, and the reception given to this famous book has shown the value of its fresh, lively ideas.

Lloyds Bank Tax Guide   Sara Williams and John Willman

An average employee tax bill is over £4,000 a year. But how much time do you spend checking it? Four out of ten never check the bill – and most spend less than an hour. Mistakes happen. This guide can save YOU money. 'An unstuffy read, packed with sound information' – *Observer*

Trouble Shooter II   John Harvey-Jones

The former chairman of ICI and Britain's best-known businessman resumes his role as consultant to six British companies facing a variety of problems – and sharing a new one: the recession.

Managing on the Edge   Richard Pascale

Nothing fails like success: companies flourish, then lose their edge through a process that is both relentless and largely invisible. 'Pascale's analysis and prescription for "managing on the edge" are unusually subtle for such a readable business book' – *Financial Times*

The Money Machine: How the City Works   Philip Coggan

How are the big deals made? Which are the institutions that really matter? What causes the pound to rise or interest rates to fall? This book provides clear and concise answers to a huge variety of money-related questions.

READ MORE IN PENGUIN

Cosmopolitan Career Guides: a series of lively and practical handbooks
produced by *Cosmopolitan* writers on a wide range of subjects.

Cosmopolitan Guide to Working in Retail
Elaine Robertson

The retailing business is the country's biggest employer, providing jobs
for one in ten of the UK workforce. What kind of career opportunities
can retail offer you? From window dresser to buyer, personal shopper
to department manager, this informative book will help you choose the
right career.

published or forthcoming:

Cosmopolitan Guide to Working in PR and Advertising
Robert Gray and Julia Hobsbawm
Cosmopolitan Guide to Student Life
Louise Clark
Cosmopolitan Guide to Getting Ahead in Your Career
Suzanne King
Cosmopolitan Guide to the Big Trip
Elaine Robertson and Suzanne King
Cosmopolitan Guide to Finance
Robert Gray